#PERIODT!!

MY GUIDE TO ENTERING WOMANHOOD

MsThomasRN

Reproductive Health
& Sexuality Educator

HOV
PUBLISHING

#PERIODT!!

My Guide To Entering Womanhood

HOV Publishing is a division of HOV, LLC.
www.hovpub.com
email: hopeofvision@gmail.com

Editing & Proofreading: HOV Publishing Editorial Team
Front Cover Design and Inside layout by HOV Design Solutions

For more information email: MsThomasRN@gmail.com

ISBN Paperback: 978-1-955107-63-1
ISBN eBook: 978-1-955107-00-0

Printed in the United States of America

MsThomasRN

The year was 1989, I was 16 and a freshman in an all-girls high school. I began dating a young man that lived in my neighborhood, and he was 18. In the beginning of our relationship, there was lots of kissing and hugging and this went on for about a year. I was a virgin, and I wasn't comfortable having sex just yet, so I didn't. My boyfriend was very patient with me but after nearly a year of dating he persuaded us to "take it to the next level". I was very nervous and very scared but a part of me wanted to have sex just as bad as he did. He was more experienced than I was and had already had sex prior to meeting me. He assured me that he knew what he was doing and that he wouldn't get me pregnant. Because I loved him I agreed, and we had sex for the first time. It was very, very uncomfortable. I did not use any protection, nor did I use any birth control. He told me about the "pull out method" and how sex felt better without a condom, so I trusted him. Sex like this became our norm and because I was still getting my period I thought we had this down pat! Well…after months of having unprotected sex I no longer saw my period, it ghosted me (SMH), and I went straight into panic mode. You see, my mom knew I was dating and would occasionally ask me if I was having sex, but I always told her "No". Well, that month I didn't get my period so there was no need for me to use sanitary napkins. I never knew my mom was keeping watch, but she was.

I had two younger sisters. One was 6 years younger than me and the other was 18 months younger than me. The older sister and I were close in age and were both going through puberty and having our periods. My mom would keep the sanitary napkins in the linen closet for us to use when we got our periods but what I didn't know was that every month she would count the sanitary pads in there. The month my period ghosted me I didn't use any sanitary napkins from the closet so there were more pads in there than there should have been. She asked both my sister and I when we got our periods, but I lied to her. She didn't say anything afterwards, so I thought my lie was good. The next day she called my sisters and I into her room with my dad present and stood us in a row, that's when I knew THINGS were about to hit the fan! She said, "One of you is pregnant and it's not your baby sister because she hasn't gotten a period yet, so she was dismissed. Now, it was just me and my other sister standing there. My heart was racing, my stomach felt twisted, and I thought I was going to die at the hands of my mother. I had to think of a plan quickly, so I began staring at my sister as if she was the one that was pregnant, knowing all along that it was me.... My sister looked at me and said, "I don't know why you're staring at me, I'm not pregnant". She ran into her room, got her calendar and showed my mother the week she got her period. I stood there in silence, trying to figure out

what I was going to say 😫 next. After my sister proved her case, she was dismissed too, so I was left standing there by myself. I was nervous as hell, and I didn't know what to say so I just stood there. It was an awkward silence for a few minutes, I guess my mom was waiting for me to start talking but I didn't. Finally, my mother broke the silence and asked me if I was going to say something. I immediately began crying and after a few moments I began to tell her my story about having unprotected sex and being pregnant. She and my dad were very disappointed in me, and I was disappointed with myself. At this time, I was now 17 and a junior in high school. This conversation seemed like it lasted for hours and at the end of it my eyes were bloodshot red from crying so much. You see, I was the oldest daughter, and I

felt like I had let my sister down. I was mad 😡 at myself and even madder at my boyfriend for "getting me pregnant", this was all his fault! After years and years, I realized it was 90% my fault that I got pregnant because I knew what could happen but didn't take the right actions to prevent it from happening. I guess I got caught slippin! ... SMH!

The next day my mom and dad called me into their room again. After speaking with each other, they told me that I was too young, not ready for a baby and still in school. My mom said she was going to take me to the clinic, and I was going to have an abortion. I knew what an abortion was, but I didn't know all that it involved. I was scared as hell and had second thoughts of not going through with it. She told me she had scheduled the appointment for a week away and that she was going to take me. After sharing this news with my boyfriend, he said he would support me with whatever decision I made. I told him I didn't want to go through with it, and I wanted to keep my baby. He said he would talk to my mom, but I begged her every day up until that appointment to change her mind. After his conversation with her, my mother told me she decided to let me keep my baby. She made it very clear to me that this was "my baby" and that I was going to finish school.

I began prenatal care, continued my school studies while I was pregnant and graduated on time. Motherhood was no joke while being a student. I watched my sister and my friend's party and have fun all the time, but I had to stay home and take care of my baby. Looking 👀 back, I have no regrets, it was challenging, but I had a supportive family and a mom who was determined not to let me fail. My teen pregnancy experience taught me some valuable life lessons about myself and my body.

After graduating high school, I decided to pursue a career in nursing. I wanted to be a nurse that taught women (mainly adolescent women) about their bodies and how to protect themselves. College was tough with a small child, but I was determined to make it. You see, I never wanted to be a statistic (a black uneducated teen mom), so I fought to NOT become her. Three years after having my son I became pregnant again with my daughter and married their father. Having now 2 children and a husband I had to put school on a back burner. A year after having my daughter our marriage failed. We were young with two children and just couldn't get it right, so we divorced, and I moved back home with my family and my two small children. I knew I had to get my life together so that I could provide for my children, so I made the decision to re-enroll back into school and complete my dreams of becoming a nurse. The road now was even tougher with two children, but I was determined to beat the odds and any negative statistics of being that young, black, and uneducated mother. After several years of college, I graduated and became a Registered Nurse.

Graduating as a Registered Nurse was my greatest achievement. It was the stepping stone of all the things that would come later in my life. My first job as an RN was with a well-known reproductive health establishment. Their focus was completely on women's wellness and reproductive health. I chose this career because I wanted to educate and empower women about their reproductive rights. I wanted to provide quality health care services, particularly to adolescents, that would have a positive effect on their lives. After nearly 30 years I kept that promise and devoted my adulthood and career to the empowerment of young women facing similar obstacles through any portal I could locate. My commitment and enthusiasm for reproductive health have allowed me to work with women of all ages, nationality and religions in my community.

This journal is dedicated to you, all the young women I have serviced and to all the women I will empower on their reproductive health.

I am MsThomas RN

PERIODT!

Heeeey Beautiful,

You are freaking amazing, and you are going to do amazing things with your life! This journal is just for you. It's a place for you to write down all your personal and most intimate feelings regarding what's going on in your body.

Going through puberty is going to be rough if you haven't already. If you're going through puberty now, I'm sure you'll be able to relate to many things in this journal. During this phase in your life, you are going to be overwhelmed with so much information about the changes happening in your body. Your friends will talk to you, you'll get information from social media sites, television and/ or the internet that may not all be true. The reason I wrote this journal for you is because I want you to get the most up to date and accurate information from me. I've been a nurse in this field for a very long time, and I've seen and done just about everything you can imagine. I am NO stranger to women's health, so I wanted to share my knowledge and what I have experienced in my years as a nurse with you.

You cannot escape puberty girlfriend. It is normal and a part of your life as you transition to womanhood. Talking about puberty, believe it or not will relieve a lot of anxiety when these changes start happening to you. I want you to be prepared before these changes even happen and comfortable when they do happen so that you are not scared, confused and /or surprised when your body starts to change.

Some of the topics in this journal may be weird, awkward or even uncomfortable as you read them but, I hope that you are receptive to this information I'm going to share with you and embrace it. If you have a mom or guardian you can talk to about puberty, I encourage you to do so. I know you may want to talk to your friend, especially if she's going through puberty as well, but remember puberty is different for everyone. Her symptoms may not be the same as yours so please don't rely on "her" experiences to be "your" experiences 😬.

It is very important for you to know about your body and why your "lady parts" are so vital 🧡 to your reproductive health.

Children's Rights

The Right to be children.

The Right to have fun.

The Right to have feelings and ideas and to express them.

The Right to ask for what they need.

The Right to some secrets.

The Right to say no.

The Right to Privacy.

The Right to make certain choices.

The Right to feel safe.

The Right to be respected.

The Right to be accepted for who they are.

The Right to know their limits.

The Right to be nurtured and cared for.

The Right to a support system, including peers.

and supportive adults.

The Rights to rewards and natural consequences.

The Right to be protected from abuse or neglect.

The Right to be believed.

The Right to a relationship with their parents.

The Right to be protected from knowledge beyond their years.

The Right not to worry about grown-up problems.

The Right to be HAPPY

(author Unknown)

Table of Contents

Hey beautiful 🤩; It's me, your Nurse. Let's talk so I can tell you some interesting and wonderful things about yourself. How well do you know yourself inside and out? Let me take you on a trip. A trip filled with everything that has to do with you and what's going on in that body of yours. I created this journal hoping it would empower and inform you about some things that are very important because it's all about you. I'm here to get all in your business girl and force you to get to know yourself better than you already do. Can I do that? 🫣 I want you to think about some serious things and I hope that all the questions you have will be answered and be clear to you after reading this journal. Let's get right into it, Fren.

Tell me a little about yourself.

_____
_____
_____
_____
_____
_____
_____
_____
_____
_____
_____
_____
_____
_____
_____
_____

Wow, you're really a dope and beautiful 🤩 female! Thanx for sharing your story with me. About 40 years ago I was just like you. I was a young lady experiencing some changes in my body and learning what was going on with me. It was a very scary 👽 experience. "Things" were happening to me, and I didn't like it, nor did I understand it. I was fortunate however because I had a mom who was very open and honest with me and helped me to understand why my body and mind were changing. I'm not sure if you have that support, but if you don't, I'm here to walk you through it, I gotchu girl! 🥰 I just need you to have an open mind about the information you're going to read throughout this journal. Take a deep breath and let's get started.

#PERIODT!!

What's the Tea About Those XX's?

Before you were made, your mom and dad came together, and your dad decided whether you were going to be a boy or a girl. Look at the two XX's genes above, these two XX genes determine that you are going to be a female. One of those X's came from your mom, and the other X came from your dad. Congratulations YOU ARE ASSIGNED FEMALE! Now if mom gave you one "X" gene and your dad gave you one "Y" gene what would you be? Take a guess? _____.

Each one of your parents gives you one of their genes and that makes up who you are. So, thank your dad for making you the person you are and thank you mom for carrying you in her body for 9 months 🤰 ....lol.

When your mom was pregnant with you, her body knew you were going to be a girl before she did. When she was 2 months pregnant with you, your reproductive system was fully developed. This means you had ovaries which contained millions of eggs 🪺 (each egg smaller than a grain of salt) (Babycenter.com). When you were born you had more than enough eggs to make a baby when you get older. Only a few of these millions of eggs will make a baby, the others will die and cause you to have a period 🩸 (blood loss) approximately every month until you get older.

#MyLadyParts
Reproductive System

Tell me what you think your reproductive system is

_____

_____

_____

_____

_____

Tell me why you think it is important?

_____

_____

_____

_____

_____

_____

_____

Did you know that your reproductive system consists of internal (inside) and external (outside) organs inside of your body? Well, if your answer was NO, let's talk about it. The main purpose of your reproductive system is to produce hormones (messengers) that make it possible for you to get pregnant and to maintain that pregnancy, of course when you're mature and old enough. Those hormones are estrogen and progesterone, and they are considered the "Female" hormones. These hormones influence your reproductive organs so that they work together to perform a certain job (for example: your menstruation, puberty and pregnancy). Some of those reproductive organs consist of your ovaries, fallopian tubes, uterus, cervix and your vagina.

Every one of these organs are important and work together to make pregnancy happen. Let's talk about them and find out what exactly each one of them does. The diagram below is a picture of what these organs look like.

Female reproductive system
Internal and external

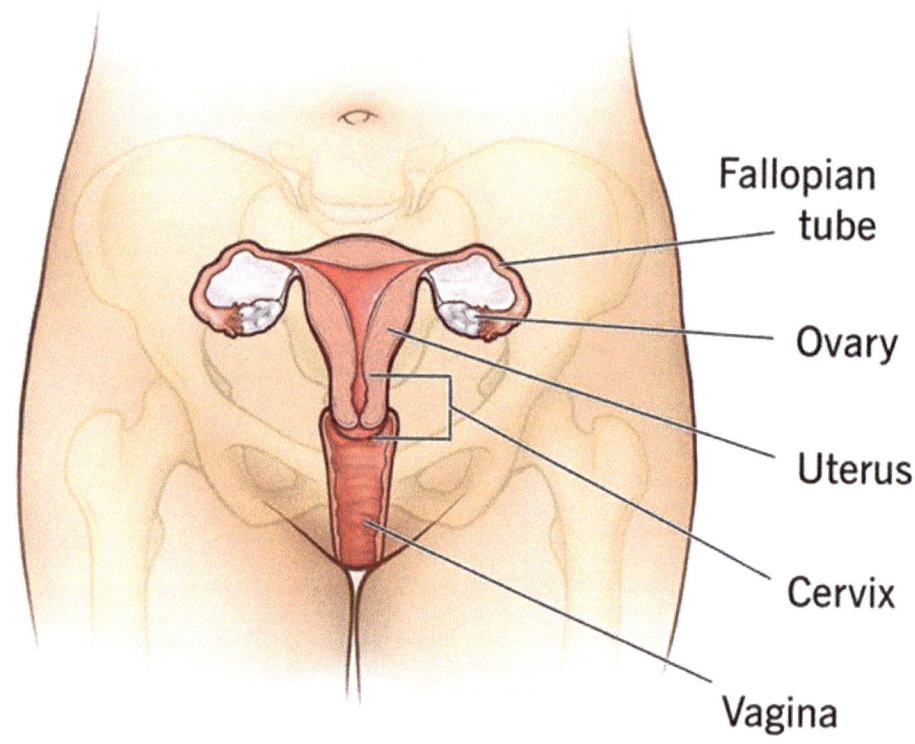

Fallopian tube

Ovary

Uterus

Cervix

Vagina

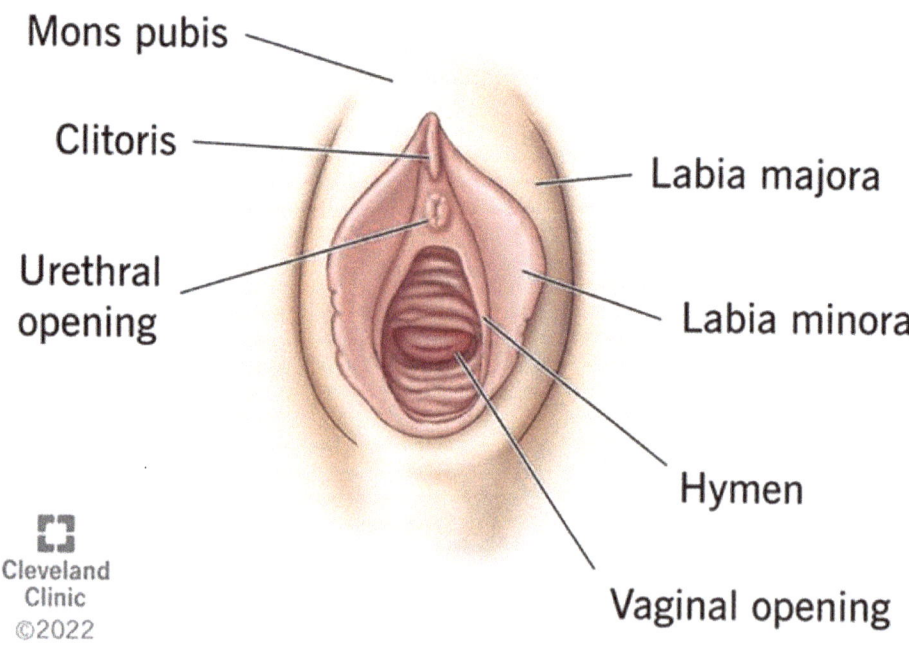

Mons pubis

Clitoris

Urethral opening

Labia majora

Labia minora

Hymen

Vaginal opening

External (Outside Organs)
My Vagina aka My Va J-J

Your vagina aka your Va J-J is a very important organ in your body, and it plays a very important part in your reproductive health. Your vagina is a very stretchy and muscular organ. Its shape is like that of a tunnel, (a dark tunnel to be exact). As an infant your vagina is very short in length but can grow up to the length of a ruler as you mature to adult womanhood.

Your vagina has three main functions:

1. Your vagina serves as a passageway (like a tunnel) for vaginal discharge and blood to exit your body when you have your menstrual cycle.
2. Your vagina receives the penis during sex.
3. Your vagina serves as a passageway for childbirth.

Fun Fact: Your vagina cleans itself. Douching (fluid inserted into vagina to clean it out) is NOT necessary!

Another Fun Fact: If you choose to have a baby in the future, your vagina can stretch as large as a bagel. The baby's head during birth is the same size as a bagel. Imagine that!

Mons and Pubis

If you look closely at the picture above, the mons (top of the vagina that resembles a mountain) has tiny hairs on it. It's covered with hair to protect the parts of your vagina and all its organs. As you go through puberty you may notice some vaginal hair beginning to grow there and it will grow thicker. Pubic hair is important because it protects the delicate skin of your vagina. It also helps to trap germs and bacteria that will try to enter your vagina. Your pubic hair helps to reduce friction from your clothing and during sex. It also helps to regulate your vaginal temperature which can decrease yeast, odor and/or other vaginal infections.

Some women choose to remove their vaginal hair. If that's something you choose to do, that is your preference. Make sure that if you do remove this hair that any razor or devices you use are clean and that you are careful not to cut yourself. A cut in this area can be very uncomfortable and can lead to infection if not treated properly. If you choose to use creams or hair removers make sure to check the ingredients so that you don't have any allergies to any of them that may cause irritation.

Make sure to bathe daily so that your vaginal hair and area are fresh and clean. If the amount of hair is too much ask your mom or use a mirror to help you trim it down.

How do you feel about shaving your vaginal hair?

_____

_____

_____

_____

My Clitoris

Your clitoris aka "the clit" or "g-spot" has one and only one function. It's a soft piece of skin that is located above your urinary opening (look at the picture and locate your clitoris). It is known as the "pleasure center" for women. When the clitoris is touched and or aroused, it can make you feel good. It is the most sexually sensitive organ in your body. You may not understand this feeling right now, but you will, if and when you become sexually active.

Fun Fact: the clitoris has thousands of nerve endings.

My Urethra

Your urethra is a small opening that is located above the opening to your vagina. Its sole purpose is to bring urine outside of your body. If you thought urine came out of your vagina, guess again because you are wrong. It does not. Urine does NOT come out of your vagina. It comes out of your urethra.

Labia Minora and Labia Majoria

Your labia minora (small) and labia majora (large) are extra folds of skin in your vulva (vaginal area). Its job is to protect the opening of your vagina and your urethra. Think of your labia as petals on a flower.

My Hymen

Your hymen cannot be seen physically. It is located inside of your vagina but can be seen on this diagram near your vaginal opening. It doesn't really serve a purpose in your body or reproductive system. It is sometimes called the "hallmark of virginity". The hymen can be torn the first time you have sex. Some women may even have a small amount of blood from the vagina the first time they have sex. You may have heard the expression "pop a cherry".

Notes

_____

_____

_____

_____

_____

Internal
(Inside Organs)

My Fallopian Tubes

Your fallopian tubes are about the size of spaghetti noodles. If you look at the diagram above, there are two tubes located on either side of your uterus. They serve as a passageway to carry your eggs from your ovaries to your uterus.

Fun Fact: The union of the sperm and egg join in the fallopian tubes, in other words, this is where pregnancy takes place.

My Ovaries

You are born with two small, oval-shaped glands that are located on either side of your uterus. Your ovaries are attached to the end of your fallopian tubes. If you look at the diagram above, your ovaries look like two cotton balls and are about the size of a small strawberry. Their function is to produce and store your eggs and make hormones (estrogen and progesterone) that control your menstrual cycle and pregnancy.

Fun Fact: According to the Centers for Disease Control, females are born with millions of eggs. However, each month thousands of those eggs will die until you reach puberty. Once you reach puberty, approximately one egg (sometimes more) will be released from your ovaries every month until menopause (the end of your menstrual cycle).

Another Fun Fact: One of your eggs is about the size of one grain of salt or sugar. Now that's small! A tablespoon of sugar or salt is an example of how many eggs you are born with, imagine that!

My Uterus

Your uterus, (a.k.a. your womb) is a reproductive organ that is responsible for many functions. It is about the size of your fist and resembles an upside down pear when you are not pregnant. When you become pregnant it stretches like a balloon and can stretch to the size of a watermelon to house a full-term baby. 👶🏾

Your uterus is also used to hold blood and tissue during your menstruation. During your menstruation, you may have cramping. This is because the uterus contracts and is pushing out blood and tissue from your body.

Fun Fact: Your uterus is the strongest muscle in your body and contracts strong enough to push out a baby. Now that's really strong!

My Cervix

Your cervix is the opening to your uterus. It encloses and protects the fetus (baby) during pregnancy and opens during childbirth. Close your eyes and imagine this. Think of a balloon that is blown up, hold the balloon 🎈 at the bottom where the knot is. That knot is your cervix. Before you can get into the balloon, you must go through the knot (cervix). When you become pregnant, that knot closes really tight protecting the fetus (baby) and all the fluid that's in your uterus from coming out until you're ready to give birth.

Fun Fact: When you have a baby via the vagina, that knot (your cervix) can stretch from 1-10 centimeters or the size of a cheerio to the size of a bagel. That's big enough for a baby to come through, side bar… "It's VERY painful too!"

My Anus

Your anus is not part of your reproductive system. It just happens to be located in an area close to your vagina. It is located at the bottom of the vagina opening between both of your butt cheeks. It is a part of your digestive system (this system starts in your mouth; your body absorbs the nutrients from the food you eat and exits the waste (poop) through your anus. Its purpose is to carry stool (poop) 💩 out of your body. Your poop contains lots of bacteria, so after having a bowel movement it is ALWAYS good practice to wipe from the front of the vagina to the back near your anus and dump the tissue in the toilet. This helps prevent feces (poop) and bacteria from getting into your vagina.

So now that we have gone through all the organs of your reproductive system what do you think? 💬

_____

_____

_____

_____

_____

_____

_____

_____

_____

_____

_____

_____

_____

_____

_____

#BecomingAWoman

Puberty

Hi Beautiful, what does puberty mean to you?

_____

_____

_____

_____

Technically speaking, puberty is nature's way of transforming your body from a child to an adult woman so that you can reproduce (being able to have children) in the future. It's a process but it doesn't happen all at once, it happens in stages. Puberty happens sometime between 9-18 years old. Your body will change in new and exciting ways and most times it can be confusing. Not only does your body change physically, but the way you think and make decisions will change and the friends you hang out with or the hobbies or activities you choose may also change. You are growing up and that is Ok!

So, what's causing all of these changes? Hormones! This transformation is possible due to hormones in your body. What are hormones you may ask? According to the CDC (Center for Disease Control), hormones are chemical messengers in your body that regulate many bodily functions and are essential for life and health. For example, as you go through puberty, you may notice that your breasts are beginning to grow or that you may have vaginal bleeding. This is due to hormonal changes in your body.

You see beautiful, you were born with ovaries, fallopian tubes, and a uterus. These important organs are necessary for you to make and carry a baby in the future. As you mature and enter puberty you start to develop these hormones in your body (estrogen and progesterone). Estrogen is the main hormone that's triggering all the changes that are happening in your body. These hormones have many effects on your body including your menstruation, growth and emotions. During puberty, you may notice lots of changes happening to you. Let's look at some of the changes you can expect at puberty.

- **Your Breast:** One of the most noticeable changes may be your breast. The estrogen hormone sends a message to the brain and tells the breast to start growing. Your breasts will slowly start to increase in size; they may even be tender during this time. Over time they will get larger and larger. Breasts are important because they will make and release milk to feed your baby if you decide to have children in the future.

- **Your Hips:** During puberty you may notice that your hips are becoming more curvy. This may be due to the weight you gain during this time. As you go through puberty your waist may get smaller and your hips, thighs and your butt will get curvier.

- **Your Height:** During this phase, you may feel like you're growing taller very fast. This is normal and all a part of puberty, you're literally "Growing Up".

- **Your Skin:** Due to your hormones, your skin may become oily. This may cause acne (pimples and /or blackheads). Acne is very common during this time and can be very overwhelming for some women. Daily bathing is recommended to prevent a buildup of oil and bacteria (the cause of acne) on your skin and especially your face.

- **Your Hair:** You may notice that other than on your head you may have started growing hair under your arms, on your arms and legs and in your vaginal area.

- **Your Hands and Feet:** Your hands and especially your feet will start growing very fast, this means larger shoe sizes.

Here are a few questions about puberty:

What changes have you noticed in your body since you started puberty?

_____

_____

_____

_____

_____

_____

What change do you like the most and why?

_____

_____

_____

_____

_____

_____

What change do you not like and why?

_____

_____

_____

_____

_____

_____

How do you feel about having acne?

_____

_____

_____

_____

_____

_____

How do you feel about going through puberty?

_____

_____

_____

_____

_____

_____

#PERIODT!

🩸 My Menstrual Cycle 🩸

Menstruation, (your period) represents a major stage of puberty for you. It's a sign that you are becoming a woman. Some young women start menstruating from as early as 9 years old and as late as 18 years old. No one knows why the age is different for some women or when this is going to happen but somewhere between these ages it may happen.

According to the CDC of 2023, "your menstruation is a normal biological process experienced by millions of women around the world each month. A period happens when the uterus sheds blood and tissue from the uterine lining leaves your body through your vagina. The start of your period is known as "Menarche." Menarche does not happen until ALL the parts of your reproductive system have matured and are working together. About once a month, a tiny egg leaves one of the ovaries (ovulation), and travels to the fallopian tube towards your uterus. During this time (usually for a month or so) your uterus fills up with thick tissue and blood. If the egg is not fertilized (during sex) the thick tissue and blood will break down and leave your body through your vagina for the next several days. This is known as your period."

Your menstrual cycle starts from the start of one period to the next period. You may find that your menstrual cycle lasts for 28 days, and some women may have cycles for as short as 24 days, while others as long as 30-35 days. Initially your cycle may be irregular (meaning you don't have a cycle every month), this is common when you're just starting your menstrual process. You may even miss a month or two, but don't be concerned. Usually after a few months your period will become normal and unique for you. This process will last for 45-55 years and then will stop permanently.

This is called menopause but that's a whole other story. For now, let's just focus on getting you through this chapter of your life... PERIODT!

The calendar below is commercial but simply represents your period and your emotions during that time. You're not CRAY CRAY your emotional - It's a hormonal thing...lol

https://www.cbc.ca/stevenandchris/m_health/your-time-of-the-month

#IrregularPeriods

Once you begin to get your period you may notice that you don't get your period at the same time every month. Irregular periods are very common, especially during the first couple of years of beginning your period. For example, you may get your period after 25 days one month and after 40 days the next month. Your period skipped a month, this is called an irregular period. Most of the time there is nothing to be concerned about. As you get older your period will adjust and get its own unique schedule.

Sometimes being sick, you're eating habits, gaining or losing weight too fast, or stress can make your period irregular. Fun Fact: the part of your brain that regulates your period also influences these events. So, relax a little, you may be the reason your period is off. IJS 😜 ...

#Amenorrhea

Amenorrhea is a condition where you don't get your period. There can be many reasons why you don't get a period. This can be caused by hormonal problems, eating habits, problems at birth and /or exercise. If you don't get a period by age 16 this may be a reason to see a medical provider.

#Menstrual Bleeding Color Chart

	Dark Red	Bright Red	Black	Brown	Gray	Pink
The start or end of your period	🔴	🔴	🔴	🔴		
Heavy bleeding during your period	🔴	🔴				
Ovulation (may be seen mid cycle of your period)						🔴
Irregular period or possible infection					🔴	🔴

Thick

Watery and thin

Jelly-like blood clots

1

2

3

When your bleeding is "thick" this is a sign of a healthy period. Usually, the first few days of the beginning of your period are red and thick. Your menstrual flow may also be heavy. It's a good idea to wear heavy sanitary napkins and carry a few extra ones so that you can change your pad when it soils.

Towards the last few days of your period, you may notice that your bleeding has slowed down, very thin and maybe even watery. This is because most of the blood and tissue have already passed through when you had heavy bleeding.

Sometimes you notice your bleeding looks like jelly or it has small clots, this is normal. These clots are dark red or dark brown and usually don't cause pain. If you have multiple clots, they are large (like the size of a quarter) and your bleeding is very heavy, you may need to see a provider. This can be very uncomfortable.

#PMS

Premenstrual Syndrome

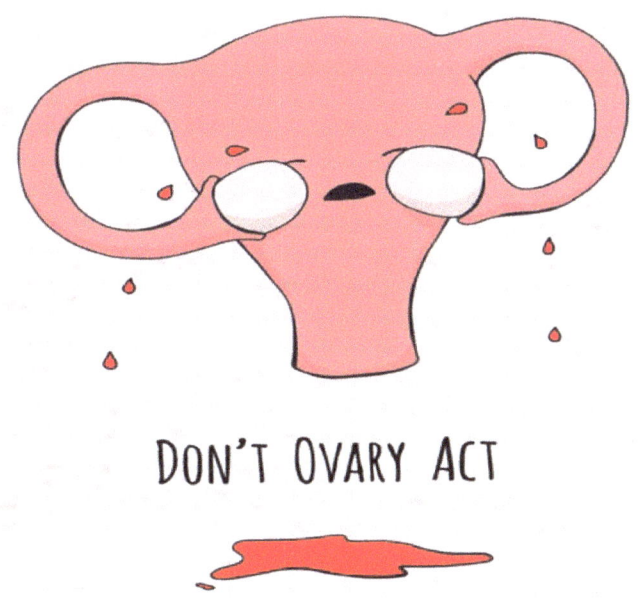

DON'T OVARY ACT

https://www.period.media/shopping/dont-ovary-act/

Premenstrual syndrome aka PMS is known as the signs and or symptoms you may experience right before you get your period or during it. These signs and symptoms don't happen to everyone and hopefully they won't happen to you. Due to the hormonal changes happening in your body, you may become very emotional or have physical symptoms. These symptoms can include moodiness, sadness, anxiety, bloating, breast tenderness, cramping and/or acne. The good news is that these symptoms usually go away after the first few days of your period.

Circle the PMS symptoms you experience?

bloating, cramping, breast tenderness, acne, constipation, diarrhea, weight gain, headaches, back and muscle pain, unusual sensitivity to light or sound mood swings, feeling depressed or irritable, feeling upset, anxious, or emotional, tiredness or trouble sleeping, changes in appetite food cravings, clumsiness, confusion, trouble concentrating, forgetfulness

_____

_____

_____

_____

_____

_____

_____

_____

_____

_____

_____

_____

_____

_____

_____

#Cramping

You may have cramps with your period especially in the first few days…. Ugggh!

Cramping is a normal part of your menstrual cycle. Some women have light cramping and others may have really bad cramping aka (dysmenorrhea). During your menstrual period, your uterus contracts to help empty out the tissue and blood from your vagina.

If cramps bother you, here are a few things you can try to soothe the discomfort. A warm heating pad applied to your abdomen feels REALLY good, and or taking medication (Tylenol or Ibuprofen) can also soothe the pain.

Most women don't have any problems with their periods but if you experience any of these symptoms below you may want to tell your mother or guardian so that they can get you the help you need.

- if cramping is severe and does not feel better after taking medication or using a heating pad.
- if your period lasts more than a week
- if your bleeding is heavy and you are soaking through a thick sanitary pad or tampon faster than an hour.
- if you have severe PMS that affects your daily activities.

My Thoughts 🔴

The Periodt 🩸 Quiz

What counts as the first day of a new menstrual cycle?

    The first day of a new calendar month

    The first day your period starts

    The first day after your period has finished

    Whenever decide when your own cycle starts as long as you keep track

Which of the following would be considered an average length of time for a period to last?

    2 days   3-5 days   6-8 days   9-12 days

What does the word "amenorrhea" mean?

    The absence of periods   Having 2 periods in one month

    An irregular cycle   Starting your periods at 8 years old or younger

What color is normal for period blood

Light pink   Bright red   Brown   All of the above

Bonus Question:

From first period to menopause, how many periods do women have on average in their lifetime?

    Around 200   Around 450   Around 800

#HygieneDuringYour
PERIODT

Blood has no odor until it leaves your body. Depending on your menstrual flow and your hygiene this can determine the smell your vagina may have. As a young lady you should bathe daily because it eliminates bad odor. If you are not able to bathe daily, at least wash your vagina area and under your arms daily to prevent odor. Bad odor can cause you to be bullied and/ or even have low self-esteem and this is not kool! Make sure to put on new underwear daily as well. If you don't have enough underwear for daily wear, wash your underwear out every day. Although you may wear sanitary napkins or tampons to catch blood from your period it may still soil your underwear. After a few hours, that blood will start to smell foul and so will your vagina area. Practicing good hygiene while you have your period can prevent a host of vaginal problems, PERIODT!

#MyThoughts

So now that you know about your menstrual cycle, what are your thoughts?

_____

_____

_____

_____

_____

_____

_____

_____

_____

_____

_____

_____

_____

_____

_____

_____

_____

#KeepitCleanKeepitClassy!

Vaginal Sanitation

Are you more comfortable using sanitary napkins or tampons? Why or Why not?

_____

_____

_____

_____

_____

What brand of sanitary pads or tampons products do you use and why?

_____

_____

_____

_____

How often do you change your sanitary napkins or tampons?

_____

_____

_____

_____

Thank you for sharing that information with me, Beautiful. Before you had to choose the product you currently use, you probably asked yourself why I need this, and which one I would be more comfortable using. This conversation is the conversation that should be discussed before you get your menses (period). Your first period (menarche) is a new experience for you and being prepared plays a major role in your experience. Now, if you haven't started your period yet, it's ok. I'm going to provide you with some information that may help you transition into this phase of womanhood. If I asked you, should you use sanitary napkins or tampons when you have your period, what would you say? You probably wouldn't know if you haven't gotten your period yet, but the fact is that when you start your period, you will need to use something to prevent the blood flow from messing up your clothing. In the world we live today there are so many sanitary products marketed to women. Sanitary pads and tampons however are the most popular. Whichever you decide to use it's really up to you and how comfortable you feel about touching your body and using these products.

Sanitary Napkins/ Pads

Sanitary pads/ napkins are the most popular to use when you're just starting your period. They are simple to use but can be costly depending on the brand you choose. Sanitary napkins are thick absorbent pads that are placed inside of your panties. As your blood flows down the napkin will be in place to catch the blood. Depending on your menstrual flow, you may want to use a heavy, medium or light sanitary pad. Your pad should be changed every two to three hours unless the flow is very heavy. You should shower daily while your menses (period) is in progress to prevent vaginal odor. It may be a good idea to wear dark colored cotton underwear (during this time only) because they are less likely to be stained from the blood and also decrease the smell of blood. Changing your sanitary napkin often decreases the smell of blood and odor. After use of each sanitary napkin, wrap up the saturated napkin and dispose of it in a sanitary way. Your menstrual flow (bleeding) has no odor until it comes out of your body. So, a nice suggestion is to put the saturated pad into a plastic Ziplock bag and then into the trash, this helps to decrease the odor of blood. As your flow gets lighter you may want to switch to a lighter pad or panty liner for the remainder of your period.

Tampons

Tampons may also be used during your menses. Some women prefer using tampons because they are discrete and can't be felt because they are inside of your vagina. Just like sanitary pads/ napkins, tampons come in small, medium and large sizes depending on your blood flow. If you choose to use tampons, you should be comfortable with touching your vagina as well as where and how to insert it. Washing your hands before inserting the tampon is important to prevent any bacteria or germs from entering your vagina. Tampons should be changed every three to four hours to prevent prolonged use unless your blood flow is heavy, if so I recommend you change it often. Just like sanitary napkins, saturated tampons can be placed in a Ziplock bag and discarded into the trash.

What happens if you are not able to remove the tampon or if you forget to remove it?

This situation may occur if you use tampons but DON'T panic! A change in position when removing the tampon may help. For example, wash your hands first then lay on your back with both knees up. Insert your fingers into your vagina and remove the tampon. If this does not work, ask your mom or a health care professional to remove it. Now of course you may feel uncomfortable with someone else seeing and touching your body but if the tampon is left in the vagina for a long period of time, it can be very dangerous and lead to a serious condition called TSS or Toxic Shock Syndrome.

According to the CDC, "TSS is a rare condition caused by bad bacteria. Prolonged tampon use and the chemical contents in the tampon can be very dangerous. Tampons should not be left in your vagina overnight or for prolonged hours (no more than four hours at a time). TSS is a serious condition but can be treated with antibiotics".

Vaginal aroma & Intimate Vaginal cleaning

You should be familiar with your natural vaginal aroma (smell) and when it is abnormal. A change in your vaginal aroma is a clue that something may be going on and needs further evaluation with a GYN provider. If this is the case, you should tell your mom or a trusted guardian what's going on so that you can get the care that you need.

A smelly vagina is caused by a mix of bacteria and sweat on your skin. This may be caused by a lack of hygiene, a change due to your hormones especially during your period, the food you eat, vaginal infections and/or sometimes medications.

To prevent vaginal odor, I recommend that you shower daily. Use mild or unscented soaps to cleanse the vagina. Limit vaginal perfumes and/or deodorants because they can cause a change in your vaginal PH, which can disrupt your "normal" vaginal smell. Wear light cotton panties because this limits moisture and odor throughout the day. Drinking water hydrates your body and helps to eliminate vaginal odor. If you are sexually active, wear condoms ALL THE TIME to prevent sexually transmitted infections. Vaginal infections will make your vagina smell very bad! PERIODT!

Douching

What is douching?

Douching is when a female rinses out the inside of the vagina using water or other mixtures of fluids. Some women douche to get rid of vaginal odor. Some women may want to douche after their period to get rid of excess blood and tissue from the uterus and that is ok. However, excessive douching can also disrupt the PH (balance) of the vagina fluids. Although douching may make the vagina smell "good" this is temporary and NOT necessary!

There may be times however when not all vaginal odors can be prevented. A smelly vagina can be a sign that something is going on, and it can be embarrassing. Don't let this embarrassment prevent you from talking to your mom or a health care provider about these concerns. You may need treatment.

Fun Fact: Your vagina does a pretty good job of cleaning itself, and douching is not necessary for routine hygiene. If you douche frequently, you can cause your vagina to be prone to vaginal discomfort because it may cause the vagina to become very dry. Daily proper hygiene (bathing) with mild soaps and washing between the folds of the vagina are all that's needed for your vagina to smell good.

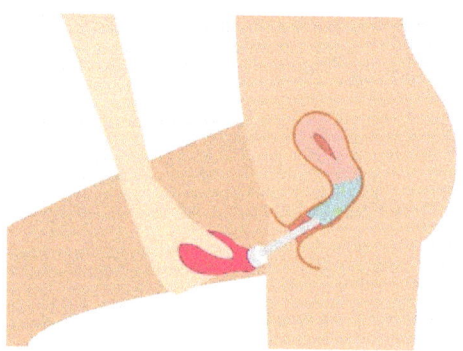

_____

_____

_____

_____

_____

_____

_____

#Acne

What the Zits!

Acne is a skin condition that causes "pimples," and it usually starts during puberty. It can pop up in many places on your body, but the most evident place would be your face. Acne is not pretty, and it may make you feel not so pretty, but it is common due to the hormonal changes happening in your body.

During puberty your body makes lots of oil to keep your skin moisturized, especially on your face. Your body and your face have lots of tiny holes (pores) that allow sweat and toxins to come out of your skin. Sometimes these pores get clogged up with oil, pus, dead skin cells which cause acne.

You may notice an increase in acne a few days before you get your period. This is called premenstrual acne which is common and may only last for a short while. Be patient, it will go away. If they should appear on your face, DON'T squeeze or pop them. It will be tempting to get rid of them, but the truth is, if you do, they can become infected and or leave a nasty mark on your face.

To limit pimples,

- avoid excessive junk food and sugars
- drink lots of water to hydrate and cleanse your skin
- bathe and wash your face daily with warm water
- avoid make-up, lotions and hair gels, this can also clog your pores on your face

If acne becomes really bad talk to your mom or a health care provider for treatment. Some medicines help prevent or reduce acne.

Having acne can cause you to feel unpretty, embarrassed or have low self-esteem. This can lead to being bullied and make you feel bad about yourself when you're around other people. Unfortunately, you may not be able to control acne all of the time but practice good hygiene, eat well and ignore the rude comments PERIODT!

What skin care products (if any) do you use to prevent acne or manage it?

_____

_____

_____

_____

_____

_____

_____

_____

_____

_____

_____

#TheGirls

My Breast aka Mammary Glands

You may be wondering, why do you have breasts? Well, most women are born with two breasts, and they are very important in your reproductive health. The main function of your breasts is to make and store milk so that you can feed your baby after giving birth. The hormones in your body stimulate your mammary glands in your breast to make milk. Somewhere between 7- 12 years old your breast may begin to 'Bud" (grow). They may be tender and sore. This may even happen before you get your period or start puberty and it's totally normal. The most visible part of your breast is the areola and your nipple. Let's talk about them.

Your areola is the dark colored circle area of your breast that covers your nipple. The areola has glands called Montgomery glands. When you decide to have a baby, these glands lubricate your nipples so that they don't get dry and crack. That would be so painful.

Your breast nipple is in the middle of your areola. Its function is to bring milk outside of your breast so that you can feed your baby. Inside of your breast are lobes (they look like small grapes). These lobes help in the production of milk in nursing mothers.

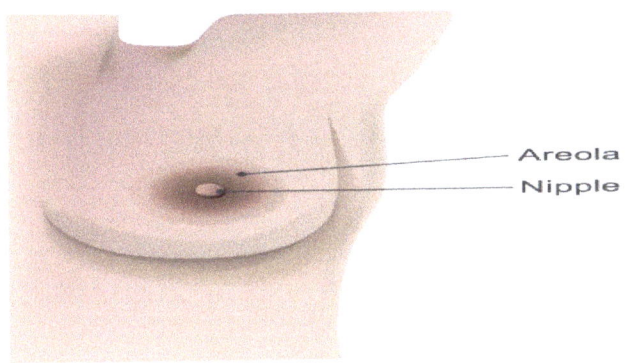

Areola
Nipple

Now that your breasts have begun to grow, a training bra may offer some support and comfort for your developing breasts. This bra keeps your breasts from bouncing (which may be uncomfortable) especially if you are involved in sports. During puberty your breasts will grow bigger, and you will start to resemble the look of a mature woman, this also means your bra will get larger.

Buying a bra can be pretty exciting or overwhelming at first. To begin, you need to know what size bra you need, so you will have to measure your breast. My suggestion to buying your first bra is to go to a store like Victoria's Secret and let them measure your breast size. A sales associate will apply a measuring tape around you. The tape will wrap from your back to the front of your breast, this will measure the width, this is known as the "band". For example: 34 A cup means that the width aka "band" size of your breast is 34 and "A" measures the cup size. The bra cup size can range from A-N or maybe bigger. Write down your bra size if you know it:

_____.

Your bra should not be tight or uncomfortable. Let's do a bra check now. Look at your bra, the hook on the back of your bra should be positioned in the center of your back, between your shoulder blades. If your bra is "riding up" your back this means your bra is TOO SMALL! If it's "sagging" it is TOO BIG! Your bra should be comfortable with BOTH breasts comfortably inside of each cup. If you don't wear the correct size bra you can damage the skin on your breast, back or shoulders. If you are unsure of the size of your bra size, you can have your breast measured at many department stores for the correct size.

Your bra should be washed after 2-3 wears. Your bra after too many wears' harbors bacteria, sweat, yeast and not to mention persistent odor! A dirty bra can cause skin irritation and possible skin infections.

Your breast during your Menses

During your menstrual cycle you may notice a change in your breast a few days before you get your period. The "girls" may feel a little lumpy, they may be a little tender or may be a little larger. These are all normal signs. These changes are due to an imbalance in your hormone level and usually go away in a few days. It's ok to massage your breast during this time or you can even apply a warm compress for relief. If they become too uncomfortable, have your mom / parental guardian make an appointment to discuss this concern with a healthcare professional.

Why do some women have big breasts and others do not?

Whether your breasts are small or large, they serve the same purpose, which is to nurse a baby after pregnancy. The size of your breast DOES NOT matter when it comes to this! There are a few reasons, however, that may contribute to the size of your breasts. One reason could be genetics. If your mom had big breasts, you may have big breasts too. Sometimes during puberty, you put on extra weight (fat) from eating and all the hormonal changes happening in your body. For some women, this extra fat can form around the breast causing an increase in size, other females not so much. Big breasts can cause back issues and can affect the way you walk due to their weight. So, for those women with small breasts don't be so quick to want huge and voluptuous breasts. Not everything that looks good is good…. LOL. Regardless of your size, all breasts are beautiful and serve the same purpose.

Why are breast exams necessary?

Take a moment to feel your girls (breast) right now. You may notice that one of them feels slightly larger than the other and this is completely normal. Most women will have their breasts with them for as long as they are alive and even after that. As you mature, your breast will change in size and in shape. Become comfortable with touching and examine your breast often, this may benefit you later on in life. When you're familiar with how your breasts feel and look, you'll know if or when something is not right. Don't be ashamed to feel your breasts, THEY ARE YOURS! A breast exam can be done by you in the shower preferably a week or so after you finish your period. This is recommended because during your period there may be some changes in your breast size and texture due to the hormonal change, so wait a few days later and then examine yourself.

How to Perform a Breast Exam on Myself

1. First thing you should do is remove your bra. You can sit on a bed or stand up, preferably in front of a mirror.
2. Look at one breast at a time. Check for any signs that are abnormal, ex: dimpling, changes in the size or shape of the breast, nipples that are inverted or any redness. These are all signs that "something" may be going on.
3. To perform a manual exam, lay on a firm surface or while standing (in the shower is a great place to do this exam). Place one hand above and behind your head. Use the other hand to gently massage your breast starting from your collar bone to your bra line and from your armpits to your ribs. Use circular motion to ensure you feel every part of your breast. Check for any lumps, knots or anything that feels different.
4. Repeat this action for the next breast.

5. If you notice ANYTHING abnormal or if you're UNSURE of what you felt, make an appointment to have your breast examined by a professional healthcare provider.

GYN exams are not only to examine your vagina, they also examine your breast as well. The provider will check for lumps, bumps, scars or anything that's abnormal. This exam is necessary to detect any breast abnormalities and to rule out early signs of breast cancer.

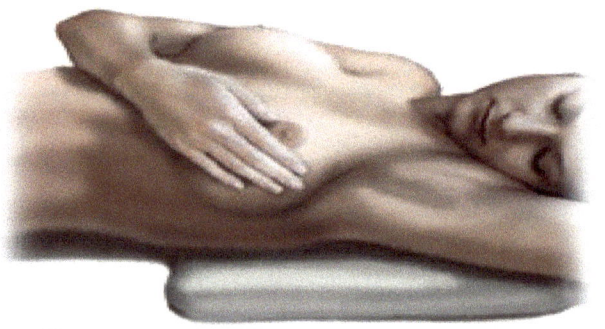

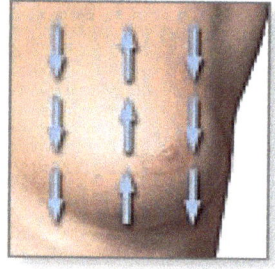

Breast self-exam:
Manual inspection
(reclining)

With fingertips close together, gently probe each breast in one of these three patterns

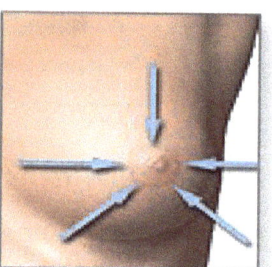

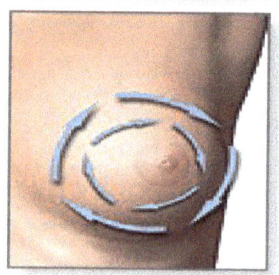

✿A.D.A.M.

_____

_____

_____

_____

_____

_____

#Summary

Now that you know a thing or two about puberty, how would you describe

puberty in your own words?

_____

_____

_____

_____

_____

_____

_____

_____

_____

_____

Puberty is normal and a healthy part of your development. It can be exciting and confusing at all at the same time. Your body will change, and it may be uncomfortable but just know that it is absolutely necessary for you to reproduce later on in life. It is important for you to know what's happening to your body so that you are prepared for the changes that will come. Embrace puberty as much as you can and don't be afraid to ask questions.

PERIODT!

The Female Reproductive System

```
X E S E I R A V O I T I N M T I N
S N I H L M R G N D N M P D J U E
E O G L R Y O O E D O X O S E F I
B R J Q X R D E O U I A Y U W H M
U E G G F A C Q K I T Y Q T S T R
T T U T E R U S P S A C Z E L U Y
N S V F E R E Q R K Z O B F V G R
A E S E O J F M P Z I D J P Y E R
I G F D V K I W N C L Z S B V U Z
P O E W U P Q O B F I X G C R W D
O R L M M C C M T Z T I O F B U S
L P K K A N I G A V R V Y P Q Y R
L V U L V A N V A F E R N S S S Y
A A S H V A Q X S L F E F T H Y O
F U E V F M B B Y R Q C F A D R S
Y U M X T N X W I V U V A A P Y R
V K T D N S R X U Z R O D C M J C
```

Fallopian tubes   Fertilization   Progesterone
Ovaries   Vagina   Cervix
Uterus   Vulva   Fetus
Ovum

Female Reproductive System

1. AYBB _____

2. IBRTH _____

3. RTSSEAB _____

4. RVXIEC _____

5. GSEG _____

6. AOFIANPLL ESTUB _____

7. ALEEMF _____

8. FTIERILYT _____

9. USTFE _____

10. SNADLG _____

11. ESRMNOOH _____

12. RBAOL _____

13. APSNUEMOE _____

14. TATNUIRSONEM _____

15. AORYV _____

16. VUOM _____

17. LETOAASPUPMSON _____

18. PCNARNYGE _____

19. UEIRVERDPOTC TMSSYE _____

20. RUSUET _____

21. VNGIAA _____

Word Bank

Fallopian Tubes	glands	baby	eggs
menstruation	hormones	labor	Ovary
birth	female	pregnancy	uterus
vagina	cervix	fertility	menopause
postmenopausal	breasts	reproductive system	fetus
ovum			

43

MY PERIODT NOTES

_____

_____

_____

_____

_____

_____

_____

_____

_____

_____

_____

_____

_____

_____

_____

_____

_____

_____

Book 2

https://www.telegraph.co.uk/family/life/parents-foolproof-guide-having-sex-talk-2021/

Keisha

Keisha was 16 years old and a junior in high school. She was an average student and enjoyed school. She enjoyed hanging out with her friends while in school and sometimes on the weekends. Of all her friends she was the only one who did not have a boyfriend so she would always be the third wheel when they went out. One Saturday Tanya, (her best friend) asked her if she wanted to hang out with some friends. Keisha didn't have any plans, so she went along. What she did not know was that Tanya was setting her up on a double date with her. She was very uncomfortable with this because she never had a boyfriend, never kissed a boy and was a virgin. After some persuasion Keisha agreed to hang out with them.

Mike was 19 years old and a high school graduate. He worked full time in the mall and was the best friend of Tanya's boyfriend. They hit it off really well. The conversation was good and Keisha thought Mike was really cute too, so they started dating shortly after. After dating for two months Keisha and Mike had sex, unprotected sex. This was Keisha's first-time having sex and she had no knowledge of birth control. She trusted Mike not to get her pregnant and for the next month he didn't. The "pullout" method was going well until it wasn't. The next month Keisha tested positive for pregnancy. She was scared and she was mad, especially at Mike because he promised he wouldn't get her pregnant. She called Mike to tell him the news, and he told her "That's not my problem, you handle that" and then hung up the phone. Keisha was even madder, more at herself because she put herself in this situation. She didn't want to tell her mother, so she called Tanya. Tanya was upset with her for not using condoms and more so for getting pregnant. She asked Keisha what she was going to do and Keisha said she wanted to abort the baby. As her best friend, Tanya agreed to go with her friend and support her through this situation.

Keisha had an abortion and was devastated that she had to go through that but was ok with her decision after some time. She was still in high school and had plans of graduating and going away to college to study psychology, so a baby wasn't in the plans for her at this time. Three weeks later Keisha returned to the doctor for a follow up. After having an abortion, a woman is advised to return to get the results of her sexually transmitted infection (STI) testing that is done at the time of an abortion. Keisha was nervous about the results but had more faith that they would come back negative. She was devastated when she found out she tested positive for gonorrhea, chlamydia, and genital herpes. She was furious at Mike and even more so when she found out he had blocked her not only on his cell but also on social media. She now had to deal with this news and this situation by herself.

Keisha turned to her doctor for help, and they discussed her treatment options. She was given medication for gonorrhea and chlamydia, however, there was nothing she could do about herpes since it is a lifelong virus with no cure. This disease is one she'd always have to live with.

There was nothing she could do but get treated, so she did. She had to live with the fact that she would have a STI for the rest of her life and that news put her in depression. Her grades began to fall, and she started skipping school causing her to fail some of her classes. Tanya was the only one who knew Keisha's story and as her best friend she stood by her side. Keisha started seeing the school therapist who was very helpful to her. She started feeling better about herself and eventually returned to school daily. Her grades even started to improve after a few months.

Four months after this ordeal happened Keisha went back to the doctor for another checkup and a repeat STI test to make sure she was clear of any infection. A week after testing she was advised to return for her results, and she did. Keisha again was very nervous but was hopeful that her tests results were negative and they were. She breathed a sigh of relief until the doctor said "but." "But what?" Keisha asked. The doctor proceeded to tell Keisha that her repeat STI testing also included a HIV test and that she tested positive for HIV. Keisha was in shock about the information she had just received and collapsed in the doctor's office. It was very hard for Keisha to accept this news, but she had to. She eventually told her mother and her mother was supportive. She began an intense medication treatment so that she could live a somewhat normal and healthy life. She graduated high school, attended college and graduated with a degree in psychology. She never had sex again; she never married and never had any children. She worked as a HIV advocate until she died at age 31.

The second half of this book is dedicated to a dear patient of mine. I decided to share her story with you so that you know how one wrong decision can change your life forever. I beg you to be smart in your decisions and to THINK before you ACT, PERIODT!

Table Of Contents

#PERIODT!!

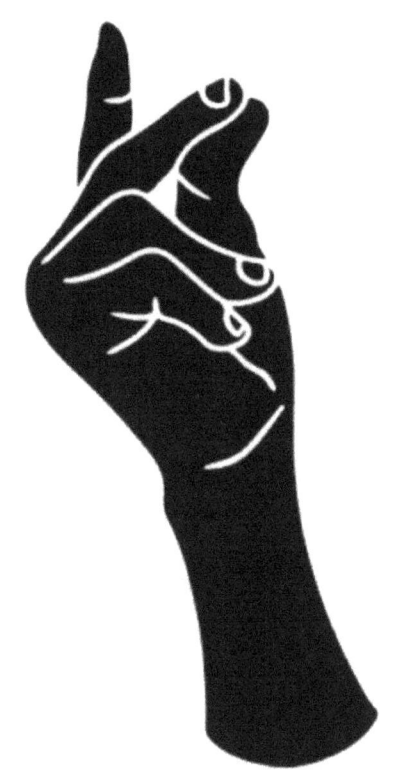

#GirlYouPoppin

Self Esteem

LOVE YOURSELF

Tell me about your self- esteem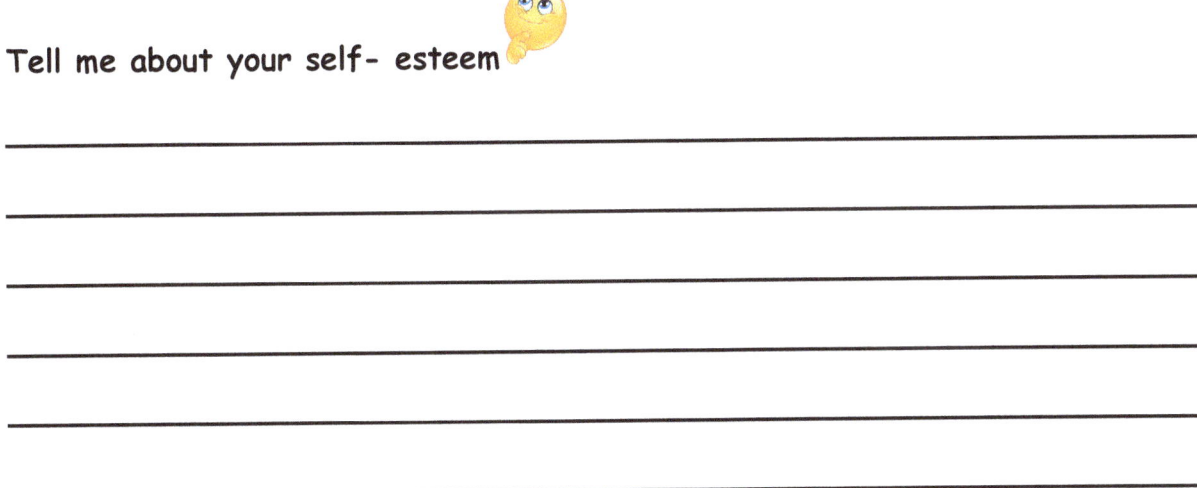

_____

_____

_____

_____

_____

_____

Thank you for sharing this information with me. Now, whether you feel like a million bucks 💵 or a bag of nickels, it's ok because after reading this book, you'll feel like the Queen👑 you are. Sometimes the crown you wear may tilt, just pause and readjust your crown but NEVER EVER EVER take it off!

What is self-esteem?

According to Webster's Dictionary if we break down the word this is what we get.

Self: You + Esteem: Respect and Admiration

If you put these words together, how you respect and admire yourself is the true definition of self-esteem. It's how you feel about yourself, your confidence, your identity, your morals and how you respect yourself. Your self-esteem starts with you as a child; however, most women are taught how to be a young lady at an early age. For example, you may have been taught to be pretty and proper in your behavior, to sit with your legs crossed, to dress appropriately or conservatively and/ or to speak politely. As you grow older, these taught behaviors may have matured with you.

How do you feel about yourself now?

_____

_____

_____

_____

_____

_____

You should be the ONLY person that makes you feel good 🥰. Never give anyone your power. You should always be confident in who you are! Esteem is also knowing what your strengths and weaknesses are. Use your strengths to make you a better version of yourself but be mindful of the areas that you need to work on for growth.

You are not perfect, and you do not need to be. You just need to be happy and comfortable with yourself. 🧑‍🦱💪

Now I want you to pause for a minute and think about 3 things that make you happy about yourself?

1. _____
   _____

2. _____
   _____

3. _____
   _____

What is low self-esteem?

Having low self-esteem is a bummer! Almost anything can cause low self-esteem, (lack of confidence, life experiences, traumatic experiences, feelings of being unloved or unwanted, etc). Any of these triggers can cause you to ignore and block the positive qualities about yourself. You may even put yourself down and use negative words to describe yourself or even begin to feel inferior to others! We may all go through this at some time in our lives, but what matters the most is not staying in this depressing space.

What would you like to work on to make yourself a better you?

1. _____
   _____

2. _____
   _____

3. _____

   _____

What is healthy self-esteem?

If you suffer from low self-esteem my heart goes out to you, but there are several ways you can turn this around. You don't have to stay in this place. You are a Queen, talk to yourself as such and rest assured the Queen in you will answer back. Here are a few confidence boosters if you need them.

- Talk positive to yourself Sis. You are a beautiful, intelligent and a dope female, don't forget that!

- Please, please, please STOP renting out the space in your head and harboring negative thoughts. You're gonna have a serious headache if you do that!

- Encourage yourself. Get outta your feelings and be your own cheerleader. Woo!

- Acknowledge your strengths and make a list. Girl, there are so many good things about you, you're the bomb!

- Stop procrastinating and get yourself some goals, girlfriend. You gotta start somewhere so let's get it moving!

- Get a hobby or do something you're passionate about. These things build up your confidence, believe it or not.

- Talk to a counselor or therapist. Learn from them, they can help you with self-management skills and techniques to help boost your confidence. I think everyone should have a therapist, get you one Sis, it will change your life! I absolutely love mine.

What are your values?

Think about your values. What are a few values that are important to you as a young lady?

_____

_____

_____

_____

_____

_____

_____

_____

_____

_____

_____

_____

_____

_____

_____

_____

_____

Values are important as you become a woman…. Why? Because having values such as self-confidence and integrity can lead to more fulfilling relationships and personal growth. This identity can empower you to set healthy boundaries, make better life choices, and foster respect from others PERIODT!

Self-love

W	I	I	U	L	S	V	L	O	V	H	O	I	A
L	O	O	L	A	I	T	O	L	E	T	O	T	E
A	V	R	S	F	B	L	R	L	I	R	L	I	C
C	A	L	T	R	E	E	L	O	I	G	Y	E	P
I	L	E	U	H	A	A	A	O	N	E	H	Y	O
G	U	F	T	F	Y	D	R	U	V	G	K	T	W
A	A	R	R	D	S	G	I	L	T	E	E	E	E
M	B	E	L	N	I	S	N	A	E	I	L	N	R
T	L	E	W	E	N	V	E	I	N	S	F	Y	F
S	E	E	D	N	G	C	I	C	R	T	S	U	U
C	R	E	A	T	I	V	E	N	C	A	L	V	L
N	T	O	Y	A	I	A	G	A	E	U	C	L	E
K	I	N	D	L	T	L	A	L	A	H	S	L	W
T	L	I	A	T	N	E	D	I	F	N	O	C	N

CONFIDENT
FREE
BEAUTIFUL
FEARLESS
LIGHT
VALUABLE
RADIANT
DIVINE
POWERFUL
CREATIVE
SUCCESSFUL
STRONG
CARING
LOVELY
MAGICAL
KIND
WORTHY

Play this puzzle online at : https://thewordsearch.com/puzzle/3773477/

Take a moment to think about why you are awesome. Fill in the blank spaces below.

Sis, you are Amazing and you better act like you know it!

PERIODT!

My Sexuality

Going through puberty is tough and it can be so uncomfortable for some women. All the physical and emotional changes can seem like a roller coaster ride. 🎢 These feelings are normal and unfortunately all part of your transition to womanhood. We tend to focus a lot on the physical changes your body goes through and not so much the emotional feelings which are equally important.

Due to the hormonal changes you're experiencing, some young women may notice a change in their confidence, feelings and emotions. You may be more sensitive towards certain things and, or people and not know how to process these feelings. You'll start to question your identity as a female and what it is that you like or dislike and who you are becoming (your identity) which is important to you. This involves your feelings about who you are attracted to. Sometimes these feelings are overwhelming and confusing, but they are normal and eventually you will figure it out. ❤️

Let's define Sexuality

Sexuality is your feelings and attraction towards someone (young men or young women) in a physical, emotional or sexual way. It's not just about sex though, it involves how you identify, how you understand and express your feelings in respectful relationships.

Sex education most times is limited to adolescent males and females. Rarely does it focus on a woman's pleasure with other women and their relationships. In this journal, I wanted to give this topic a safe space to discuss how you may feel if this relates to you. It can be really hard to process these feelings. Feelings of being isolated, embarrassed or looked down on after "coming out" can affect your life. 😰

Love is love ❤️ and who you love and desire to be with is your choice PERIODT! If you're interested in girls that may not necessarily mean that you are a lesbian and being interested in boys doesn't mean you're straight. It means that during puberty these thoughts and attractions are heightened and can be intense for some women. These thoughts are a way for you to sort out your sexual feelings and that's ok.

Think about your sexuality, what does it mean to you?

_____

_____

_____

_____

I found some questions online that I wanted to include in this journal. I thought about the young ladies who are struggling with this. These questions DO NOT define you but rather make you think about your feelings if you're unsure of your identity. These questions can be found at

https://www.wikihow.com/Relationships/Sexuality-Quiz

1. Do you ever fantasize about being intimate with someone of the same gender as you?

   A. Yes, I do fantasize about that regularly.

   B. Yes, but rarely.

   C. No, I never do. It doesn't seem appealing to me.

   D. I'm not sure.

2. How would you feel if someone of the opposite gender leaned in to kiss you?

   A. I'd be aroused and really excited to kiss them back.

   B. I think I'd be interested, but I'm not totally sure.

   C. I'd be uncomfortable and not interested.

   D. I'm not sure.

3. Whose bodies (girls or boys) do you pay the most attention to when watching movies and shows?

   A. People of the same gender as me.

   B. People of the opposite gender as me.

   C. People of both genders.

   D. I don't usually pay any attention to people's bodies in the media I watch.

5. If an attractive person of the same gender started hitting on you, how would you feel?

   A. Excited and even aroused.

   B. Curious to explore where it leads.

   C. Definitely uninterested.

   D. I'm not sure.

6. Does the idea of hanging out with another girl seem sexually appealing?

   A. Yes, I've enjoyed that experience in the past. I would love that.

B. I've never had that experience before, but I'm definitely curious to see if I like it.

C. No, I don't want to hang out with someone of the same gender.

D. I'm not sure.

7. At a party, who would you enjoy flirting with all night?

A. Someone of the same gender.

B. Someone of the opposite gender.

C. Either gender sounds great.

D. Someone I like, but I probably wouldn't want the flirting to lead to anything more than that.

8. When you think of physical attraction and intimacy, which gender comes to mind first?

A. My gender.

B. The opposite gender.

C. It depends, sometimes it's my gender and other times it's the opposite.

D. No one (or, unsure).

9. Do you find guys and girls equally attractive?

A. No, I find guys much more attractive.

B. No, I find girls a lot more attractive.

C. Yes, I find both to be equally attractive, or at least it's close.

D. I'm not attracted to either gender.

There is no score to these questions. The purpose of these questions is to help you if you are struggling with your identity.

Your Thoughts

_____

_____

_____

_____

_____

_____

_____

_____

_____

_____

_____

_____

_____

_____

_____

_____

#V-Card

My Virginity

According to Merriam-Webster, "A virgin is a person who has NOT had sexual intercourse." Some would describe sex as the penis penetrating the vagina. Choosing to have sex (losing your virginity) for the first time is a big deal. If and when you choose to have sex make sure that it is something you want to do and not pressured into doing. Your consent is needed 100% of the time, remember that.

If you are a virgin, there is absolutely no reason for you to be ashamed. The fact that you're a virgin means that you've probably thought about all the things that could go wrong if you were not prepared and that's a smart way to think. Stay in control, don't be pressured into having sex, take your time, and move at your own pace.. Don't have sex until you are absolutely ready, it's not a race. Besides, once you start having sex, you may feel different emotionally especially if you had sex with someone you were unsure of. Sex should be a special connection between two responsible people. Here are some things you should take into consideration when it comes to having sex for the first time.

1. Have you had a conversation about sex with the other person?
2. Is this person someone you consider worthy enough to share your body with?
3. What are you going to use to prevent an unwanted pregnancy and/or a sexually transmitted infection?
4. Is the environment a safe place to have sex?
5. Have you guys visited the clinic to make sure you're both negative of STI's?

Sex for the first time may be uncomfortable for some women. Most times the female is penetrated with a male's penis, and this may cause friction and irritation to your vagina. Due to the sensitivity of your vaginal skin, it is also possible for the skin to possibly tear, which can cause discomfort later on. Some women may even bleed due to the hymen being broken, (the hymen is considered the "hallmark of virginity").

Whether you choose to stay a virgin or not, please remember that your consent is ALWAYS necessary when it comes to someone else touching your body. You are in control. PERIODT!

Your Thoughts 🫣

_____

_____

_____

_____

_____

_____

_____

_____

_____

_____

_____

_____

#SelfRestraint

Is dry humping, kissing and /or cuddling with someone you like considered

abstinence behavior? What do you think and why?

_____

_____

_____

_____

_____

Sexual abstinence is a decision and the practice of choosing NOT to engage in sexual activity (vaginal penetration, anal penetration and or oral sex.) It is a way to avoid the many risks that come with sex. This decision can help you to stay focused on your school studies, future goals and things that are important to you in your life.

It is also the best practice for birth control as per, MsThomasRN because it prevents an unwanted pregnancy. It also prevents you from coming in contact with any sexually transmitted infections. Abstinence takes LOTS of will power because during puberty the change in your hormones can cause you to be very curious about sexual feelings Peer pressure can be #CRAZY! It's easy to get "caught up" because you want to be a part of the "It Girls" but staying focused is even cooler, PERIODT!

What are your thoughts on abstinence and how do you feel remaining abstinent

until you are older and mentally mature to have sex?

_____

_____

_____

_____

_____

_____

_____

Have you ever been pressured into having sex with someone? If so, how did

you handle/cope with that?

_____

_____

_____

_____

_____

_____

_____

_____

_____

_____

#ImFeelingMyself
Masturbation

Masturbation can be a very uncomfortable conversation for some women to talk about. The truth is that most people do it! Now that your body has begun to transform, masturbation allows you to learn your anatomy (your body) as well as detect when/ if something is going on in your body.

According to Webster's Dictionary, "masturbation is sexual stimulation of one's own genitals for sexual arousal or other sexual pleasure, usually to the point of orgasm". The stimulation may involve hands, fingers, objects, sex toys such as vibrators or combination of these. It is the act of enjoying self-pleasure without feeling guilt or shame. 🙄

You are probably asking yourself if masturbation is normal? The truth is that it may be for some and perfectly fine for others. If I can be transparent, masturbation is a part of your sexuality. It is perfectly okay to touch your body, after all it belongs to you and it's your body! Touching your body in a pleasurable way allows you to understand what makes you feel good. Masturbating can help you to relieve life related stressors and most importantly it's safe.

My Feelings/ Questions / Concerns about masturbation: 🫣

_____

_____

_____

_____

_____

_____

_____

_____

_____

_____

_____

_____

_____

_____

_____

_____

_____

_____

_____

_____

#SomethingsFishy

Abnormal Vaginal Discharge

Your vagina produces a liquid secretion that is normally white or yellowish in color and is very thin. This discharge is normal and is a sign of good vaginal health. These colors may change depending on the changes during your menstrual cycle and/or for other reasons. For example, several days before your menstrual period begins, you may notice that your vaginal discharge is thicker than normal. It is a good idea that you pay attention to what your discharge looks like every day, this way if something is abnormal, you'll know. If your discharge is any color other than white, it may be possible that you have a vaginal bacterial infection and should seek GYN care for further evaluation. Your vagina may also have an aroma that is "normal" to you. It should not have a pungent odor if you bathe daily. If it does, this is another reason to seek care, something may be going on.

Is there anything abnormal about your vaginal discharge?

_____

_____

_____

_____

_____

_____

Abnormal vaginal discharge can make you feel uncomfortable, physically and mentally. Tell someone so that you can get the care you need. Never be ashamed or embarrassed, this is a part of becoming a woman and you're not alone, PERIODT!

Let's talk about a few common but abnormal vaginal secretions and infections.

Most common vaginal infections

Bacterial Vaginosis aka BV

According to the CDC, "Bacterial Vaginosis is an infection caused by an overgrowth of "bad" bacteria that normally live in your vagina. When this happens, this leads to an imbalance in the vagina. Symptoms may include increased vaginal discharge that may be dark in color, a fishy 💠 odor, vaginal irritation and/or burning 🔥 ." This may make you very uncomfortable and will need attention right away. I recommend that you tell a trusted adult and have them bring you to a health professional for further evaluation.

There are ways to prevent recurring bacterial vaginosis. Probiotics (pills that contain lactobacillus) are great. They are effective in maintaining your vaginas normal smell. Fun Fact: Yogurt is a great source of lactobacillus. Avoid using vaginal hygiene products that are scented. As I stated earlier, your vaginal odor is unique to you and if the aroma is foul and unpleasant seek attention. Using scented hygiene products may smell good but they may also mask the problem you may have and/or make it worse. 😡

Yeast Infection:

According to the CDC, "a yeast infection is an overgrowth of Candida fungus. This is caused when there is a disruption of good bacteria and an overgrowth of yeast." Yeast thrives in dark and damp places. To help prevent yeast infections you should shower daily, make sure to dry your vagina thoroughly when it has been wet, wear cotton underwear and change your pad or tampons several times during the day when you have your period. Symptoms of a yeast infection may include, thick "cottage cheese like" vaginal discharge, itching and /or burning. These symptoms also warrant further evaluation with a GYN provider. But don't worry, yeast infections are treatable with antifungal medications that you can purchase right over the counter. This medication prevents the overgrowth of vaginal yeast.

Trichomonas:

According to the CDC, "trichomonas, aka "trich" is a common sexually transmitted infection caused by a parasite (a tiny organism that feeds off a host). This parasite 🐛 is passed from one person to the next during unprotected sex. It causes the vagina to have a foul-smelling odor, discolored discharge, itching and/ or burning. Sometimes it causes pain when you urinate and if left untreated can put a pregnant woman and her baby at risk. This is a serious infection that can be prevented. If you are sexually active, I HIGHLY recommend that you use condoms ALL OF THE TIME PERIODT! If you happen to become infected, you will need to see a GYN provider for evaluation and treatment. Treatment includes antibiotic therapy and abstaining from unprotected sex.

So, what's the bottom line? You may come in contact with one of these vaginal infections in your lifetime. PAY ATTENTION to your vagina and what comes out of it. If you notice any change in the color of your vaginal discharge, any abnormal vaginal odor, and/or a change in vaginal consistency, seek help right away.

My Thoughts 🧐

_____

_____

_____

_____

_____

_____

_____

_____

#PelvicExams

Pap Smear

Before we begin, tell me what you know about a pelvic exam aka Pap Smear:

_____

_____

_____

_____

_____

_____

_____

_____

A pelvic exam is also known as a Pap Smear. You may have not had this exam just yet but, this exam will become a frequent test (recommended yearly) as you enter womanhood. Pap Smears are important and necessary for your reproductive health. It is done to examine your reproductive organs, screen for cancers (HPV and cervical cancer, etc), check and treat sexually transmitted infections and to detect pregnancy.

When should you have your first pelvic exam?

When you should have your first pelvic exam depends on a few things. Some providers suggest that women between the ages of 16-18 should have their first exam. However, once you become sexually active, routine exams are highly recommended. If you are experiencing any vaginal discomfort, it might be a good idea to be evaluated by a GYN provider as well.

What happens before the Exam?

Having your first vaginal exam may be uncomfortable for the first time. Your GYN provider will examine and touch your vagina. Let's STOP for a minute!

How do you feel about this?

_____

_____

_____

_____

Before your exam you should let the GYN provider know your reason for your visit and inform them this is your first exam as well as your feelings. There are male and female providers, and you HAVE THE RIGHT to choose the provider you feel comfortable with, PERIODT! If the provider is a male, you can request to have a female staff member in the room with you. That is your choice and that is your right.

Most women prefer to schedule their Pap Smear for the time when they will not be bleeding. Some women have their Pap Smear during their period. However, doing this can possibly impact your test results especially if bleeding is heavy. Whichever you choose is your choice.

Be sure to shower before the exam, do not engage in any sexual activity or douche 1-2 days prior to the exam, and do not apply any vaginal deodorants because it may alter the test screening results.

What happens during a pelvic exam?

This exam can be very uncomfortable, especially for the first time. When you enter the exam room you will be asked to remove your clothing including your underwear and put on a gown. When you're ready you will be introduced to the provider that will conduct your exam. He or she will ask you to lay on the table and put your heels in the stirrups that are located on either side of the exam table. Stirrups are used to support your position (legs opened) on the table. This position opens the vagina and allows the provider to have visual and physical access to your vagina.

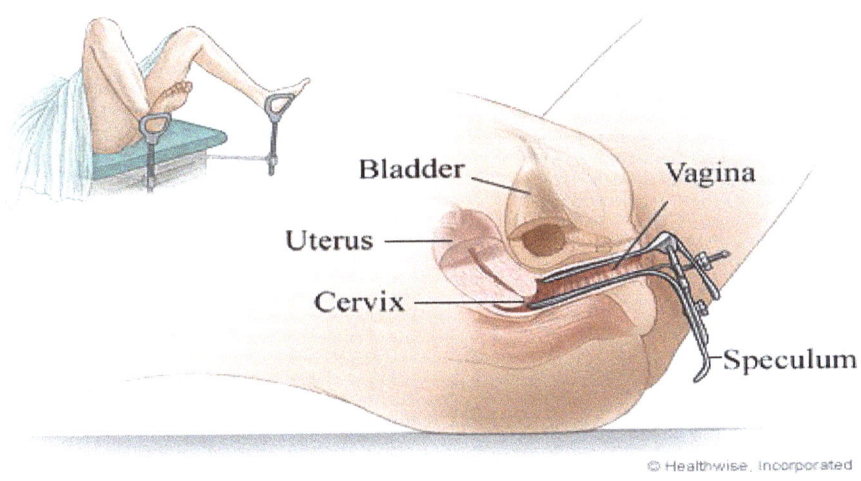

First the vulva (outside of your vagina) will be examined. Next the provider will place a plastic or metal speculum in your vagina. This speculum allows the provider to visualize and examine the inside of your vagina and your cervix. If the speculum is uncomfortable let your provider know. The exam is quick, and the provider will do their best to make you comfortable. A sample of your vaginal secretions will be collected from your cervix with a small brush or cotton swab and tested for cervical cancer.

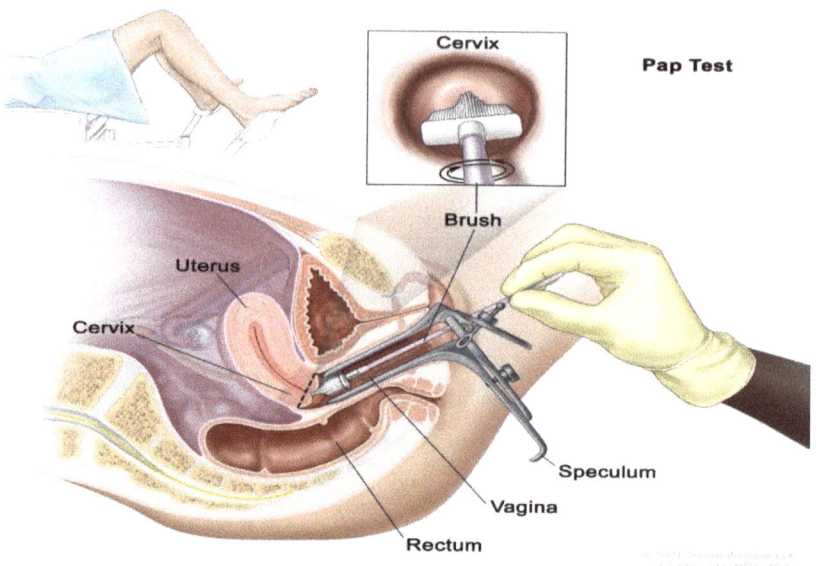

Other than routine vaginal exams, you should have a pelvic exam if:

- You have any vagina discomforts (itching, burning)
- You have abnormal vaginal odor (fishy smell)
- You have heavy vaginal bleeding or bleeding in between your periods
- You have painful cramping before, during or after your period
- Sex is painful
- You have any signs of pregnancy or sexually transmitted infection
- You haven't gotten your period by age 16.

What happens after your vaginal exam?

After your exam you will be asked to get dressed so that you can consult with your provider and ask any questions you may have. Your provider will let you know if they saw anything that is of concern ex: (rash, abnormal discharge or smell), prescribe you with medication or schedule you for a follow up exam to make sure the issue is resolved.

FYI…. It is normal to have some light spotting (bleeding) after your Pap Smear if you don't have your period. When the provider collects cells from your cervix, this may cause a little irritation and bleeding. Don't be alarmed, this is normal, and it should not be painful. The bleeding is temporary and may go away in a few hours. For this reason, it may be a good idea to bring a panty liner with you afterwards.

This chart below contains a few questions that you should be familiar with. These questions may even be asked on the questionnaire given to you at the doctor's office and prior to your exam. This information provides the provider with clues about your reproductive and medical history. This information is important to ensure that you get the best care possible.

_____

_____

_____

_____

_____

_____

_____

_____

_____

_____

_____

_____

_____

_____

_____

_____

_____

_____

_____

GYN Questions for you

Here are a few questions to note before your exam:

My GYN provider's information	
My first GYN is scheduled for	
What is the reason for this exam?	
What age did you get your first period?	
How many days does your period last?	
Do you have any cramping during your period?	
Is your bleeding heavy during your period?	
Are you sexually active?	
Are you interested in birth control?	
Are you pregnant or have ever been?	
Do you have any medical conditions?	
Do you have any allergies?	
Have you had any surgeries?	

Use this space for any other questions you can think of

_____

_____

_____

_____

_____

_____

_____

_____

#Smash

Sex

Let's start with this question. What do you think the purpose of sex is?

_____

_____

_____

_____

_____

_____

The biblical purpose of sex is for a male and female to reproduce. Others may say the purpose of sex is to relieve sexual stress. The answer to this question is different for everyone. Some women may be ready as teenagers and others as older women. Some may not want to ever have sex and that's ok. It's all up to you and how comfortable you feel about it. Making the decision to have sex for the first time can be overwhelming and difficult. Whatever decision you make, your decision should be YOUR choice, and you should not be PRESSURED or FORCE into having sex with anyone without your consent PERIODT! Sex involves physical, mental and emotional feelings with the other person. There are many important decisions that come with having sex and if you're not prepared to make these decisions, it's probably best that you wait until you are.

If you are having doubts about your decision, you're probably not ready. Let's be clear, having a DESIRE to have sex is not the same as being PREPARED to have sex.

What are your thoughts about Sex?

_____

_____

_____

_____

_____

_____

_____

_____

Before you decide to have sex, ask yourself if you have all the information you need about sex. Here are a few questions to think about:

1. How well do I know this person and do I really want to have sex with them?
2. How do I protect my health from possible disease?
3. Am I knowledgeable about safe sex and condom use?
4. What happens if the condom breaks?
5. Will sex be painful the first time?
6. Am I comfortable with someone seeing me naked and touching my body?

These questions are important to your physical health and should be very important for you to consider in your decision. If you were uncomfortable asking yourself or answering any of these questions maybe you should really take some time to think about your decision and you should probably WAIT to have sex.

Choosing to be sexually active is a decision that is very important, and it can affect the rest of your life especially if you make the wrong decision. If you decide to become sexually active, I highly recommend you protect yourself from unwanted pregnancy and disease. Protecting yourself during sex can allow you to enjoy sex especially when you are responsible and ready. Protecting yourself means a few things:

Choose the right partner. Girl, just because he/she "looks good" doesn't mean they are good for you IMJ! 😳

The person that you decide to have your first sexual relationship with should be someone that is special to you. It should be someone that you care about and someone that you trust with your mind, your heart, and your body. Make sure that you are mentally, emotionally and physically okay with your decision.

Once you and your partner have decided to have sex, both of you should visit the local clinic and both of you should be screened and tested for any sexually transmitted infections prior to having sex. Just know, the right person will be okay with this, remember his or her health is just as important. Just because you get tested and are given negative results does not mean that you still shouldn't use condoms. It just means that if the condom breaks or it falls off, you and your partner will not come in contact with any sexually transmitted infections, because you are both clear of any of those.

Once you have been tested, your next step should be to get on some type of birth control method, even if it's just a condom. Birth control plus condoms adds a double layer of protection against diseases and unwanted pregnancy.

If you have decided to have sex keep in mind that sex can be uncomfortable or even painful the first time, are you prepared for that?

Here are a few questions about sex for you to think about:

Are you or any of your friends having sex? If so, how does this make you feel?

_____

_____

_____

_____

_____

Have you ever been asked to watch porn (people having sex with each other) and if so, how do you feel about that? If not, what was your reaction to this question?

_____

_____

_____

_____

_____

_____

How would you react if someone you liked asked you to have sex with them?

_____

_____

_____

_____

_____

Are there any questions you are uncomfortable with when it comes to sex?

_____

_____

_____

_____

_____

_____

_____

_____

#KnockedUp
Pregnancy

When you go through your menstrual cycle there is a phase that is called ovulation. During ovulation your ovaries release an egg in preparation for pregnancy. This usually occurs a week to a week and a half before you get your period depending on your menstrual cycle. This egg travels to your fallopian tubes and hangs out there for a few days. This egg is patiently waiting for a sperm to come along so they can hook up (fertilization).

Now, if you have unprotected sex and you're not on birth control, the sperm can hook up (fertilize) with the egg and begin to produce a baby. This means you WILL NOT have a period for the next 9 -10 months aka pregnancy. 👶

If the sperm and egg do NOT meet, the egg travels down to your uterus and it begins to shed and break down along with the lining of your uterus. This is better known as your PERIOD 🩸. This also means YOU ARE NOT PREGNANT! Wooo Chile!…. lol.

There is no sure way to know when you may ovulate so it's always best to practice safe sex at all times. Don't get caught slippin PERIODT! So now that you know how pregnancy happens and how to prevent it, let's talk about birth control, but first…

What's Your Thoughts?

_____

_____

_____

_____

_____

_____

_____

_____

_____

How do you feel about teen pregnancy?

_____

_____

_____

_____

_____

_____

_____

_____

_____

#DontGetCaughtSlippin

Birth Control

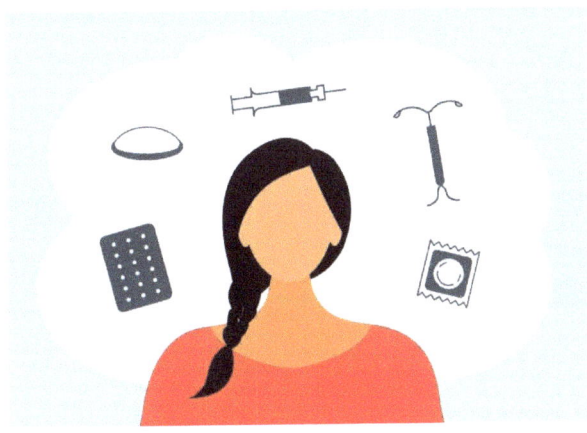

health.clevelandclinic.org

How does Birth Control work? Let's make this plain and simple! Estrogen and Progesterone are the "female hormones" in your body and they play a huge part in your reproductive health. These two hormones are responsible for preparing your body for pregnancy (menstrual cycle and ovulation) and also maintaining that pregnancy. If you do not wish to become pregnant, taking birth control can prevent that from happening by altering your body's chemistry.

Protecting yourself during sex prevents unwanted pregnancy. Contraception, a.k.a birth control is used to do just that. There are several types of birth control, you just have to decide what works for you. To begin, you should do some research on what you are interested in and then have this conversation with a trusted guardian or healthcare professional. You should always keep in mind that even though most birth control methods are safe and highly effective they are NOT 100% proof. This means condom use is highly encouraged as a second layer of protection. You may have to try several methods of birth control before you find the one that's right for you. Let's talk about a few of them but first let's talk about what doesn't work

Pull out Method......

SMH!!!!!... If a guy tells you that he'll pull out right before he ejaculates (cums) so he doesn't get you pregnant, DON'T BELIEVE THIS HYPE!!!!!. This method is NOT effective in preventing pregnancy. Before a male fully ejaculates, there are some sperm that escape from the penis, they are called "precum". Precum sperms are very smart and sometimes make their way through your body without you even knowing. They are sneaky and their goal is to race to the egg and fertilize it. It doesn't take many of them for this to happen, only one out of a million is needed. In fact, if I had to guess, lots of pregnancies have resulted from the "pull out method", maybe even you.....lol. Even if he ejaculates close to your vagina and not in, it's still possible to get pregnant. Sperm have tails and can swim 💦 faster than any Olympic swimmer... lol.

I don't care how horny you may be, if you are not on birth control and/ or don't have condoms, STOP 🔴 the show and go home. "Pull out method" WILL NOT WORK out well for you. You can thank me later. PERIODT!

If a guy refused to wear a condom and told you that he would "pull out" right before he ejaculated, WHAT WOULD YOU SAY OR DO?

_____

_____

_____

_____

_____

_____

_____

_____

Non Hormonal Birth Control

Non hormonal contraception is birth control that does not contain hormones. This means it will not disrupt your menstrual cycle. Let's talk about a few:

Condoms

The most popular type of birth control is a condom. If used correctly it can provide protection against unwanted pregnancy and sexually transmitted infections. Most clinics, schools and community-based programs provide condoms for free but if you had to purchase them, they are accessible and available in most stores. Although condoms are applied to the male penis, it also is your responsibility to make sure that they are available when needed and that they applied correctly. Condoms should be used EVERY TIME you have sex.

A Possible side effect of using condoms is latex allergy. If you feel vaginal irritation and/or discomfort after using condoms, speak to a healthcare provider, you may have a latex allergy. If this is the case lambskin condoms can be used. They are more expensive and less accessible, but they work to keep you safe. Don't get caught slippin PERIDOT!

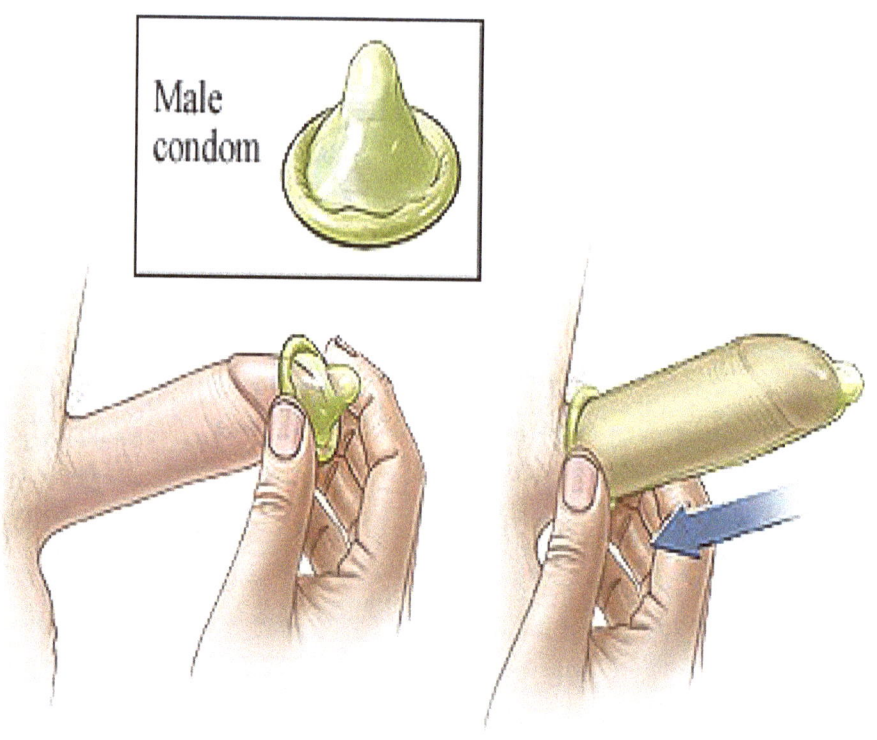

© Healthwise, Incorporated

This picture demonstrates the PROPER way to apply a condom.

_____

_____

_____

_____

_____

_____

Here are some questions about condoms. Take a minute to read and think about them, then answer them honestly. Remember this is your journal and a safe place for you to express your feelings.

For young women that are sexually active, do you think it is their responsibility to supply condoms before having sex or the young man's responsibility and why?

_____

_____

_____

_____

_____

Would you be comfortable asking a guy to put on a condom before sex?

_____

_____

_____

What would you do if a guy refused to put on a condom before having sex?

_____

_____

_____

_____

Do some research and write down a few places here where you can get free condoms if you need them?

_____

_____

_____

_____

_____

www.dreamstime.com

Intrauterine Device (IUD) is a T-shaped copper device that is inserted into your uterus via your vagina. It is inserted by a healthcare provider in a hospital or local clinic. This device does not contain hormones and is highly effective in preventing an unwanted pregnancy. The copper in this device makes it difficult for the sperm to get to the egg. This IUD can be left in the uterus for up to 10+ years and removed anytime (by a healthcare provider) when you are ready to conceive (have a baby).

Birth Control Intrauterine Devices (IUD)

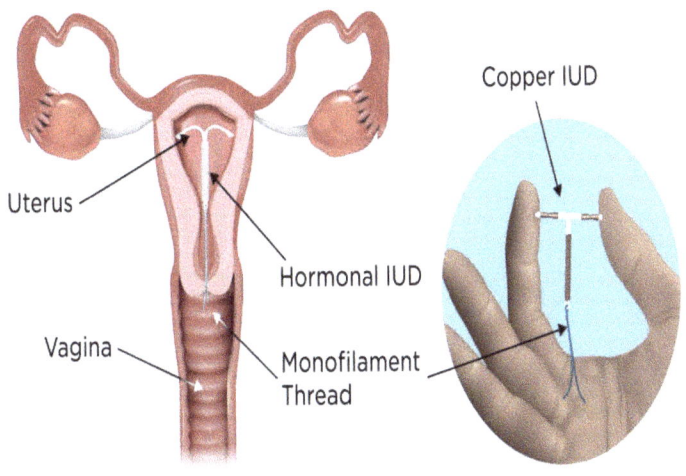

Uterus

Copper IUD

Hormonal IUD

Vagina

Monofilament
Thread

https://mydoctor.kaiserpermanente.org/

Hormonal Birth Control

Hormonal birth control works by preventing the release of your eggs from your ovaries and by changing your vagina's mucus, making it very thick near your cervix so that sperm can't get through. This prevents the egg and sperm from starting a pregnancy. These methods are highly effective if you use them AS PRESCRIBED and are only prescribed by a healthcare provider. Condoms should also be used as a second layer of protection. Here are a few types of combined hormonal birth control:

Birth Control Pills are the most common of this group. To be effective against pregnancy, they must be taken EVERYDAY Sis. One suggestion to remember taking these pills every day would be to put an alarm on your 📱 cell. It is strongly advised to use condoms with this method to prevent STI's (sexually transmitted infections).

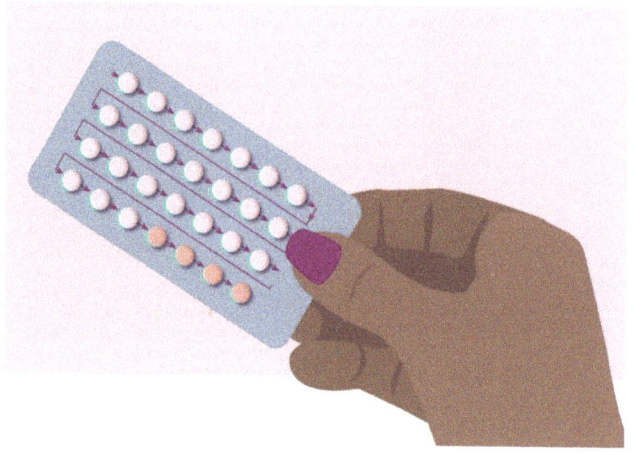

https://www.healthywomen.org

Would you try birth control pills as a form of birth control, why or why not?

_____

_____

_____

_____

What's the tea on birth control pills, good or bad, what have you heard about using them?

_____

_____

_____

_____

Birth Control Patch

Birth Control Patch is applied to your skin, and the medication is absorbed into your body. The patch must be replaced every week for 3 weeks and in the 4th week you will get your period. Unlike the pills you only have to remember to apply the patch once a week. Condoms are highly recommended when using the patch as well to prevent the spread of STI's. The patch is only available via prescription.

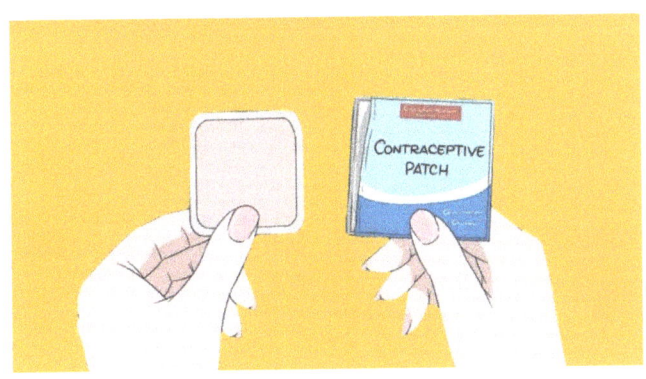

https://www.sienahealth.com/

Birth Control Ring

To use this birth control method, you have to be very comfortable with touching your vagina. This device has to be inserted into the vagina. Unlike the pills and the patch, the ring stays in place for one month at a time to prevent an unwanted pregnancy. The ring is discreet, and no one will know you have it except for you and whoever you tell. Condom use is recommended, and it is only available via prescription.

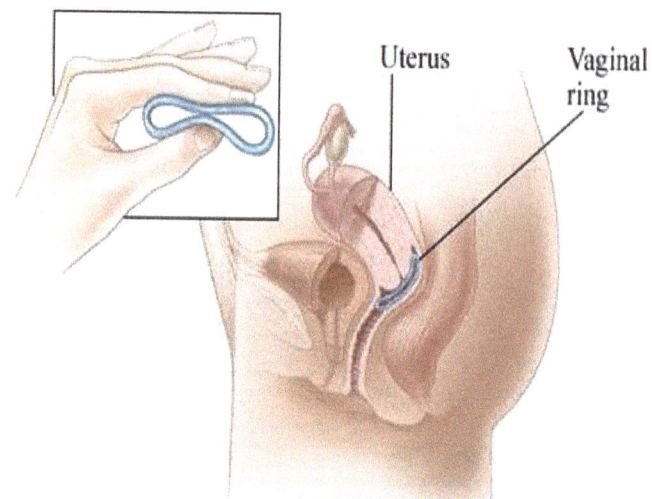

Uterus

Vaginal ring

Would you try the vaginal ring for birth control? How comfortable would you be using this method?

_____

_____

_____

_____

_____

_____

Depo Provera Injection

This method is given by injection into your muscle once every 3 months. You must go to a clinic or hospital to have this injection given. The progestin hormone in Depo prevents ovulation. This means you will not release any eggs from your ovaries, which prevents a pregnancy from happening. No one will know you are using this birth control unless you tell them. Condoms are also recommended with this birth control.

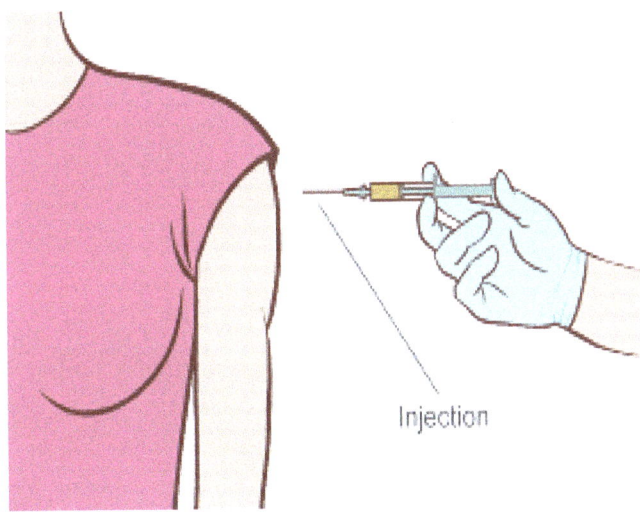

Injection

Your Thoughts 🤔

_____

_____

_____

_____

_____

_____

Emergency Contraception

Most birth control methods are effective if used correctly. Some women may not want to take hormonal birth control and use condoms only. If there is a "break" in use or inconsistency while using birth control you can also put yourself at risk of getting pregnant. If this should happen Emergency Contraception (Plan B) or (the morning after pill) can be used to prevent an unwanted pregnancy. Plan B is emergency contraception that is only intended for emergency use if taken with 120 hours (5 days) of unprotected or failed birth control use. This medication is NOT to be used as a birth control method; it will NOT work the same. Plan B can be purchased over the counter without a prescription and is available in most pharmacies.

Plan B aka Emergency Contraception

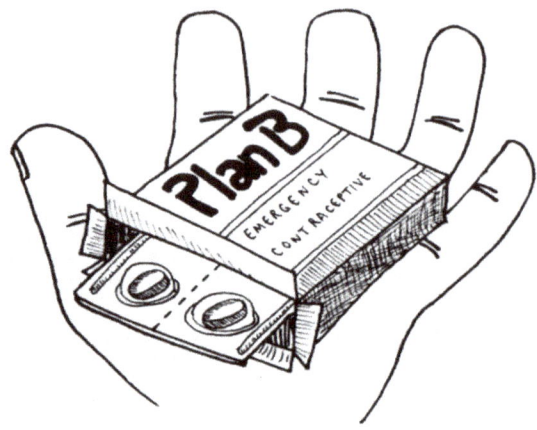

https://bowdoinorient.com/

So now that we have talked about birth control and preventing pregnancy,

what are your thoughts?

_____

_____

_____

_____

Which type of birth control would you be interested in if or when you decide
to become sexually active and why?

_____

_____

_____

_____

#YouBuggin

A sexually transmitted infection (STI) is an infection that you get from a person who already has an infection during sex. Most times you won't know if a person is infected because the person may not have any visual symptoms. Sometimes they do not even know they are infected. Therefore, it is VERY important to protect your health and wear condoms if you are going to be sexually active.

There are some STI's that are treatable and there are some that are not. They can affect your reproductive system, causing challenges and/or complications bearing children when you are ready. Let's talk about a few of these STI's.

Sexually Transmitted Infections that are Curable

Chlamydia is a common STI that can cause infection among both men and women. It can cause permanent damage to a woman's reproductive system. This can make it difficult or impossible to get pregnant if it's not treated.

Gonorrhea is another common STI. It affects the mucous membranes of the reproductive tract, including the cervix, uterus, and the fallopian tubes in women and the urethra in women and men.

Syphilis is a bacterial infection usually spread by sexual contact. It starts as a painless sore. The most common symptom may include a rash on the palms of the hands and the soles of the feet. Symptoms come and go but it is treatable with antibiotics.

Pubic Lice is commonly called "crabs." They are tiny insects found in the genital area, and they can cause itching and irritation. They are treated with a special shampoo and shaving of your genital area.

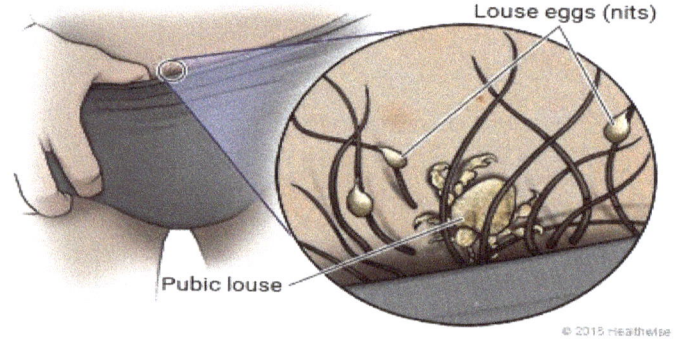

Scabies is a very contagious, and itchy skin condition caused by a tiny burrowing mite. They spread quickly through close physical contact.

Sexually Transmitted Infections that are NOT Curable

According to the World Health Organization "Human immunodeficiency virus (HIV) is an infection that attacks the body's immune system. Acquired immunodeficiency syndrome (AIDS) is the most advanced stage of the disease.

- HIV targets the body's white blood cells, weakening the immune system. This makes it easier to get sick with diseases like tuberculosis, infections and some cancers.
- HIV is spread from the body fluids of an infected person, including blood, breast milk, semen and vaginal fluids. It is not spread by kisses, hugs or sharing food. It can also spread from a mother to her baby.
- HIV can be treated and prevented with antiretroviral therapy (ART). Untreated HIV can progress to AIDS, often after many years."

HIV/AIDS is a deadly disease. If you are going to be sexually active PLEASE PLEASE PLEASE use condoms ALL OF THE TIME!!!!! Although there is no cure, HIV/AIDS is PREVENTABLE! Protect yourself and your body.

Herpes is a STI that is spread during sex if you come in contact with an infected person's sores, blisters, body fluids and/ or skin. Once the virus enters your body, it will remain there FOREVER. Occasionally it will manifest itself as a blister or cold sore on your body. It can be extremely painful especially in the vaginal area. There are two types of herpes and both are equally contagious:

1. Oral Herpes aka a cold sore is seen on your lip and is often contagious during kissing and /or oral sex. It is physically unpleasant to look at but fortunately it is temporary and can go away with medication.
2. Genital Herpes is spread through sexual contact with someone that is infected. Medication can reduce the amount of outbreaks you'll have

BUT…. Herpes is a LIFELONG infection which means even when you don't have symptoms, the virus will ALWAYS remain in your body.

To prevent Herpes infection, you should always use condoms, limit the amount of people you have sex with and most important AVOID having sex with someone if you see ANY genital sores on their body. Here is a picture of what herpes look like.

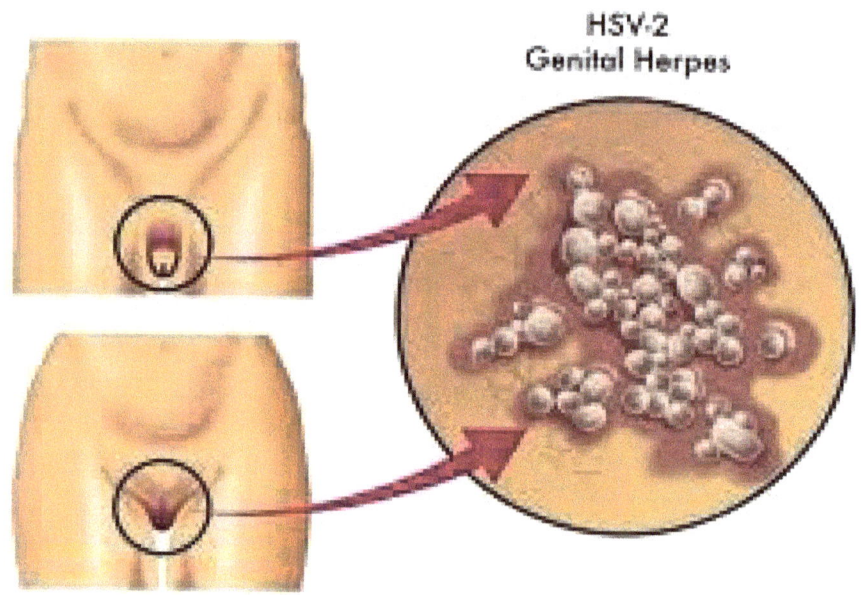

diag.vn/en/std/genital-herpes/l

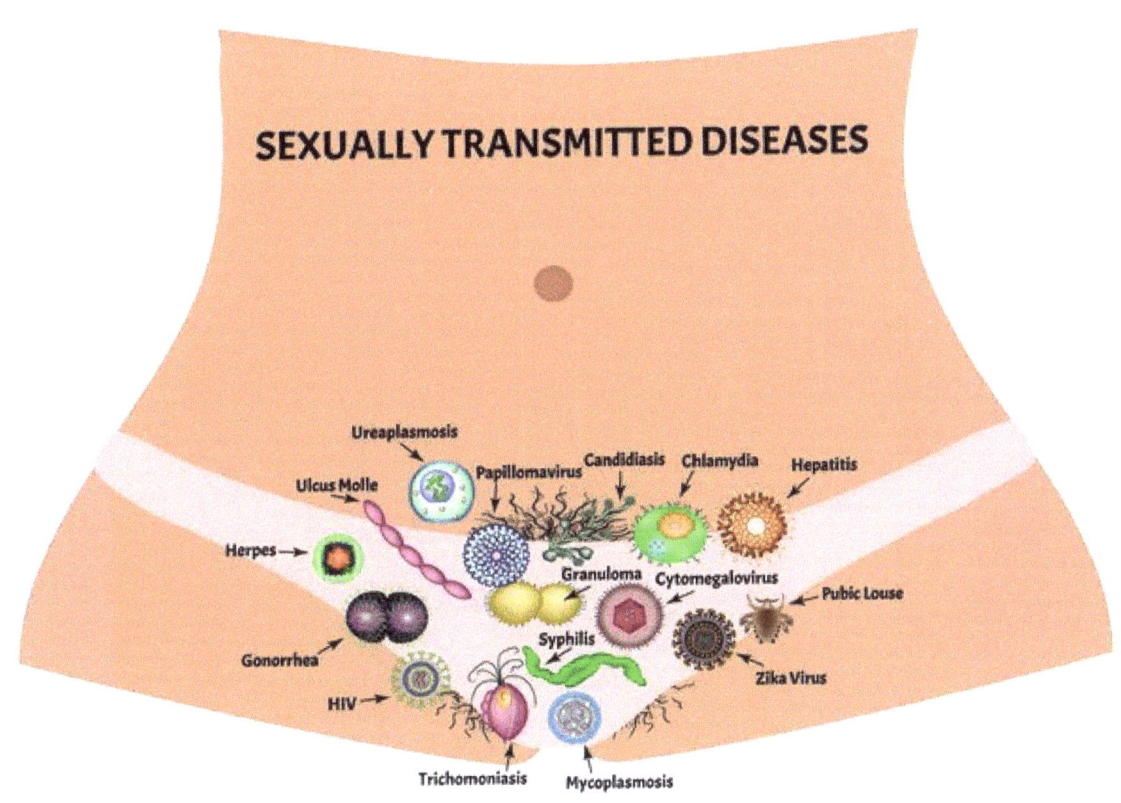

SEXUALLY TRANSMITTED DISEASES

deposithphotos.com

Your Thoughts on Sexually Transmitted Infections

_____

_____

_____

_____

_____

#Violated

Sexual Violence/ Rape

According to the CDC, 2024 rape or "sexual violence is sexual activity when consent is not obtained or freely given. It impacts every community and affects people of all genders, sexual orientations, and ages. Anyone can experience or perpetrate sexual violence.

Researchers know the numbers underestimate this problem because many cases are unreported. Survivors may be ashamed, embarrassed, or afraid to tell the police, friends, or family about the violence. Victims may also keep quiet because they have been threatened or do not think anyone will help them."

Rape is NEVER ok! If you are forced or pressured into having sex and you are NOT ok with it, please tell someone immediately. If you don't report rape it can have a negative impact on your life later on. It can disrupt your feelings, emotions, your physical health and/ or your mental health.

Pregnancy or STD exposure is possible after a rape, report it and seek medical attention ASAP! You have options and you don't have to pay the cost of this trauma.

Avoid negative behaviors and people that are associated with them. The list below are examples of negative behavior:

1. **If the vibe around you does not feel right, that's a red flag. The person does not want to give their name**
2. **Guys that want to take you home or to an exclusive place**

3. Online dating can be very dangerous. Investigate the person, meet the person in a public place and NEVER NEVER ever give them your personal information.
4. Be weary and always ASSUME they are Catfishing you especially on social media sites. DO NOT send explicit pictures of you to anyone!
5. Guys that are verbally or physically aggressive and make you feel uncomfortable.

Sex Trafficking

The purpose of sex trafficking is sexual exploitation. This means a perpetrator manipulates or forces a person to engage in different sex acts for the purpose of obtaining money. An example of sex trafficking would be a pimp and a prostitute.

Incest

According to Merriam Websters Dictionary, the meaning of INCEST is sexual intercourse between people so closely related that they are forbidden by law to marry; Incest in any form is WRONG, it is a CRIME and it is a violation of your rights as a child.

Molestation

According to Merriam Webster's Dictionary the word Molestation means to pester, bother or annoy. When a person is molested it is considered a crime because it involves engaging in sexual acts with young children. **This can include: touching their private parts, exposing their private parts, taking nude pictures of their private parts or engaging in ANY sexual activity with a minor.**

Sexually Harassment

Sexual harassment is not cool. It is unwanted and /or offensive behavior. It is a form of bullying that can make you feel really bad about yourself. Imagine someone making sexual jokes about you or your sexual orientation, spreading sexual rumors and then posting them or pictures of you on social media for fun and "likes." These people may even be bold enough to tell you to your face how they feel. Sexual harassment can really affect your life as a teen. It can disrupt your concentration, especially in school, causing low grades, missing classes and sometimes even dropping out of school. It can cause a disruption in your sleep, depression and, or anxiety.

The CDC states, "Changing social norms, teaching skills, empowering girls and women, and creating protective environments can help prevent and reduce sexual violence. We all have a role to play in prevention.

No means No!

https://www.nsvrc.org/statistics

Who can you talk to if you've been violated?

_____

_____

_____

_____

_____

_____

_____

_____

_____

_____

_____

_____

_____

_____

_____

_____

#Bruh

Boys and Puberty

Only females and males can mate and reproduce with each other. In order for the human race to continue it is necessary for human beings to procreate. Now that you understand your body and its importance, understanding the male human body is equally important for this reason.

Although this journal is for you it is important to know what boys go through during puberty. When both of you get older you will need each other in order to reproduce! So here is some informative information for you.

Just like you boys go through puberty at an early age, and many changes happen in their body as well. These changes are due to the male hormone called "Testosterone." Just like girls, boys are born with reproductive organs. The two main organs consist of a penis and two testicles which are located outside of their body. The anatomy of their body is much different from yours.

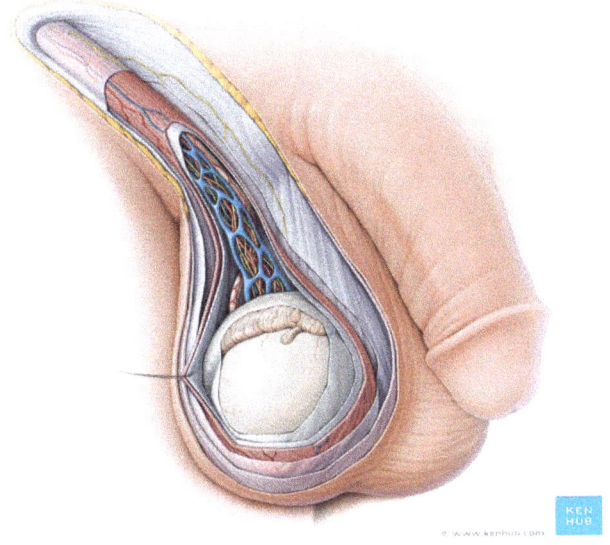

The Penis is a very sensitive organ in the male's body. Its purpose is to bring urine outside of his body and to deposit sperm into the woman's body during sex to produce a baby.

The testicles are located behind the penis, and its function is to produce sperm. Most males are born with two testicles. The diagram below shows the stages of development and maturity a male goes through when puberty starts.

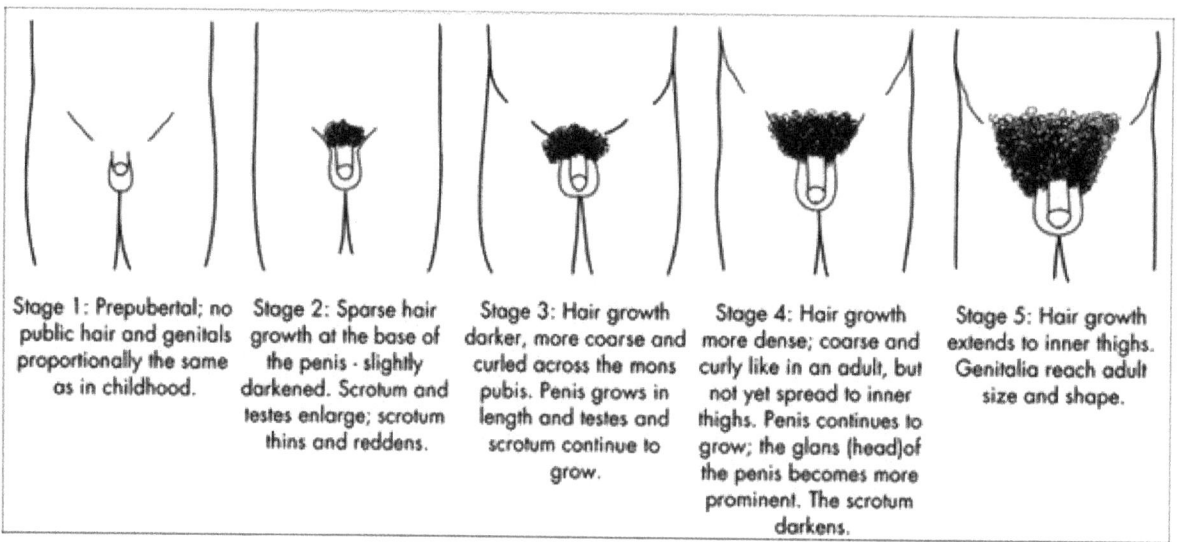

Stage 1: Prepubertal; no public hair and genitals proportionally the same as in childhood.

Stage 2: Sparse hair growth at the base of the penis · slightly darkened. Scrotum and testes enlarge; scrotum thins and reddens.

Stage 3: Hair growth darker, more coarse and curled across the mons pubis. Penis grows in length and testes and scrotum continue to grow.

Stage 4: Hair growth more dense; coarse and curly like in an adult, but not yet spread to inner thighs. Penis continues to grow; the glans (head)of the penis becomes more prominent. The scrotum darkens.

Stage 5: Hair growth extends to inner thighs. Genitalia reach adult size and shape.

Physical changes in boys usually start around age 13. Here are the changes most boys will go through during puberty.

- Their penis and testicles will grow larger.
- They may have a "Wet dream" while sleeping
  A wet dream in a boy is similar to a girl getting her period. When a boy ejaculates for the first time this means he can produce a child. Fun fact: a male can ejaculate millions of sperms at a time.
- Their voice will change and get deeper.
- They will begin to grow pubic, facial, and underarm hair and
- Their body may start to fill out with muscle.

Males are an important part of the reproduction cycle. Just like you, they experience mood swings, acne, peer pressure and may be sexually active. Knowing how the male body operates is important for you to know as well. PERIODT!

#Summary

Hey Beautiful

Let me start by saying you are beautiful, and you better always remember that! Don't EVER let anyone tell you different!. Puberty is scary and it will be an uncomfortable time in your life. You are going to question your appearance, your moods, and your thoughts, but do your best to embrace the changes and make the RIGHT choices. You will be tempted to go against your morals and your beliefs, stay strong! You don't need to participate in any behavior that makes you uncomfortable just so that you can fit in with the "In crowd." Focus on what's really important like your educational and life goals. These goals will take you further than anyone in the "In crowd."

I wrote this book because I wanted to be intentional about empowering you as you transition into this phase of your life. Having a healthy conversation about puberty is important to your health and wellbeing and it will help you deal with the changes positively and may help you feel secure. Puberty is normal and a natural part of growing into the beautiful woman you will become. Remember this, you are a Queen, empower and invest in yourself and NEVER EVER EVER be ashamed of who you are.

PERIODT!

MsThomasRN

#MyThoughts

_____

_____

_____

_____

_____

_____

_____

_____

_____

_____

_____

_____

_____

_____

_____

#MyThoughts

#MyThoughts

_____

_____

_____

_____

_____

_____

_____

_____

_____

_____

_____

_____

_____

_____

_____

_____

#MyThoughts

_____

_____

_____

_____

_____

_____

_____

_____

_____

_____

_____

_____

_____

_____

_____

#MyThoughts

_____

_____

_____

_____

_____

_____

_____

_____

_____

_____

_____

_____

_____

_____

_____

_____

#MyThoughts

_____

_____

_____

_____

_____

_____

_____

_____

_____

_____

_____

_____

_____

_____

_____

Explore the full series by MsThomasRN

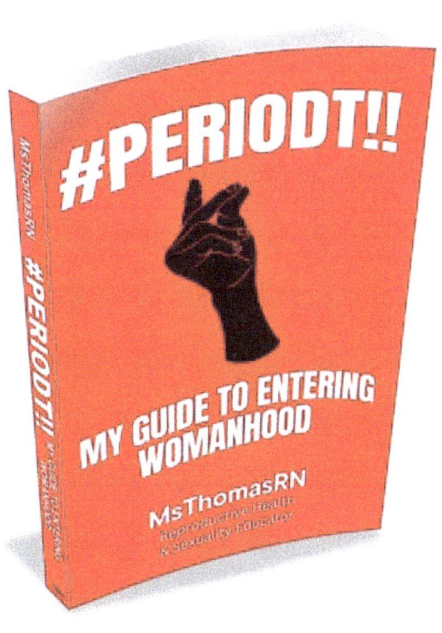 

Give your son or daughter real, relatable, and medically accurate guidance from a certified Reproductive Health & Sexuality Educator who keeps it honest and empowering.

www.ingramcontent.com/pod-product-compliance
Lightning Source LLC
Chambersburg PA
CBHW041118120626
46547CB00019B/2752